DATES AND DREAMS

Also By The Author

Words in Passing (poetry)

Last Exit to East Hampton, Prose Poems

Resurgius, a Sixties Sex Comedy

Stories, Etc.

Manhattan Spleen, Prose Poems

A Portable Chaos, Rev. Ed. (novel)

The Ideologues (poetry)

The Journey and Related Poems

Reflections in a Doubtful I (poetry)

Carbons, a Career in Letters

Fortune Island (novel)

Time and Fevers (poetry)

A Fable & Other Prose Poems

Scenario for Scorsese (novel)

Paradise Square (novel)

Murderer's Day (poetry)

50 Poems

The Poor Boy and Other Poems

DATES AND DREAMS
Short Fictions, Prose Poems, Cartoons

E. M. SCHORB

with an introduction by
X. J. Kennedy

HILL HOUSE **NEW YORK**

Copyright © 2016 E.M. Schorb. All rights reserved. This material may not be reproduced in any form, published, reprinted, recorded, performed, broadcast, rewritten or redistributed, except for brief passages used for purposes of review, reference, and example, without explicit permission of E.M. Schorb. All such actions are strictly prohibited by law.

ISBN: 978-0-692-67740-7

Cartoons by the Author

Hill House New York
Printed in the USA

Acknowledgements

Most of the poems in this collection appeared in two somewhat recent books and an earlier chapbook. The books are: *Manhattan Spleen*, Aldrich Press, 2014, and *Last Exit to East Hampton*, Kelsay Books, 2015. Poems in the chapbook, *A Fable and Other Prose Poems*, are listed below

Grateful acknowledgment is given to the Lannan Foundation and the Provincetown Fine Arts Work Center, the Ludwig Vogelstein Foundation, and the North Carolina Arts Council, for Fellowships in Literature, the financial awards from which provided the time and freedom to produce many of these pieces; and to the following publications in which they first appeared. Thanks also to Robert Rauschenberg and Change, Inc. for a grant for drawings, illustrations, cartoons.

Dedication: For Patricia, published as No Angel in *Spring: The Journal of the E.E. Cummings Society*
Commissioned to Write a Prose Poem ~ *The California Quarterly*
The Castle ~ *Spring: The Journal of the E.E. Cummings Society*
The Red Shift ~ *The Mississippi Review* (Special Issue: ed. by Julia Johnson)
The Fire Eater ~ *Sulphur River Literary Review*
The Lost Watch ~ *WordWrights Magazine*
No Miracles ~ *The Baltimore Review*
Stopover ~ *Terminus*
The Sex of Water ~ *The North American Review*
A Successful Marriage ~ *5 AM*
What the Dead See ~ *The Asheville Poetry Review*
The Sinister Clothesline ~ *The GW Review*
The Emotion Factory ~ *Illuminations*
They are Here ~ *The Kit-Cat Review*
A Thinker ~ *Illuminations*
Subjects in Mirror ~ *Mudfish*
The Aquarium Man ~ *RIO: A Journal of the Arts*
The New Green Carpet ~ *The Willow Review*
Instructions on How to Walk ~ *WordWrights Magazine*
Five Forevers ~ *Spring: The Journal of the E.E. Cummings Society*
Wings ~ *Ginosko Literary Journal*
Looking at Statues ~ *The Chariton Review*
Green Bile ~ *The Chariton Review*
Para is Normal, Not Para ~ *The Chariton Review*

At the Gate ~ *The Literary Review*
Butch, the Body-Finder ~ *Clark Street Review*
Mother in the Aquarium ~ *Untitled: A Magazine of Prose Poetry*
The House Made of Soap ~ *WordWrights Magazine*
The Care & Handling of the Horned Toad ~ *RIO: A Journal of the Arts*
The Coyote People ~ *Slant*
Footnote to a Travel Guide ~ *The Chariton Review*
The Mall on the Moon ~ *The Potomac Review*
The Bowel Organist ~ *The Spoon River Poetry Review*
The Opera ~ *The Brooklyn Review*
The Campers ~ *Quick Fiction*
Pigeons at the Post Office ~ *The Kit-Cat Review*
The Crow and the Scarecrow ~ *The Seattle Review* (longer version), *Fugue* (shorter version)
A Triangle of Lights ~ *The Southern Poetry Review* and *Poetry Salzburg Review* (Austria)
The Magician ~ *The Literary Review*
Inspiration at the Art Gallery ~ *The Birmingham Poetry Review*
Snowbound ~ *The Prose Poem* (ed. by Steve Wilson) and, in another form, *The Carolina Quarterly*
Guns and Roses ~ *Untitled: A Magazine of Prose Poetry*
What I Did on My Summer Vacation ~ *The Kit-Cat Review*
An Experiment in Governance ~ *The Mississippi Review* (Special Issue, ed. by Julia Johnson) and *Best American Fantasy*
Transformations ~ *The Wisconsin Review*
At Heart, Speed ~ *Ginosko Literary Journal*
Reaching the Top ~ *5 AM*
Pollock ~ *Envoi* (England), *Kobisena* (India)
Like the Titanic ~ *Envoi* (England) and *The Pembroke Magazine*
The Moving Finger ~ *The Haight Ashbury Literary Review*
Manhattan Spleen ~ *Gulf Coast*
Ready to Walk ~ *The New Laurel Review*
The Quick of Scent ~ *The Chiron Review*
Love and a Locksmith ~ *Caveat Lector*
The Final Tithe ~ *Gargoyle*
Signs ~ *The University of Windsor Review* (Canada)
The Rainbow Man ~ *Main Street Rag*
AND/OR ~ *Spring: The Journal of the E.E. Cummings Society* and *The Arts Journal*
Nothing Forever ~ *Writers' Forum*

Last Exit to East Hampton ~ *Oxford Poetry* (Magdalen College UK)
    and *The Milo Review*
Provenance ~ *Poetry Salzburg Review* (Austria)
The Busy Angels ~ *Lucid Rhythms*
The Careless Man and the Philosopher ~ *Cease, Cows*
The Chutist ~ *A Fable and Other Prose Poems*
The Deciduous Strip ~ *Epiphany Magazine*
Envoi ~ titled Good Morning, *The Outrider* (Australia)
Pour les Oiseaux ~ *Great American Poetry Show, Vol. 3*
The Responsibilities of a Muse ~ *Ginosko Literary Journal*
The Rubber Church ~ *South Carolina Review*
Silvamoonlake ~ *Summerset Review, Mad Hatter's Review*
The Tuba Man and the Enormous Diva ~ *A Fable and Other Prose*
    Poems
Spindrift ~ *Ginosko Literary Journal*
The Plan ~ *Poetry Salzburg Review* (Austria)
The Murder of Garcia Lorca ~ *Poetry Salzburg Review* (Austria)
Humans, Peace, and the Rumor of War ~ *Main Street Rag*
The Martyr ~ *Futures Trading Anthology Two*
The Dog Show ~ *Potporri*
Death Row ~ *The Baltimore Review*
Confessions ~ titled Scenario for Scorsese, *Long Island Quarterly*
Wilder than Wilder ~ *The Laurel Review*
The Wake ~ *A Fable and Other Prose Poems*
The Urn ~ *St. Sebastian Review*
The Terrible Shadow ~ *Main Street Rag*
Rousseauvians ~ *Cease, Cows*
Poweritus ~ *Main Street Rag*
The Genius Flight ~ *A Fable and Other Prose Poems*
Manners, Manners ~ *Futures Trading Anthology Two*
Me and My Shadow ~ *Bare Fiction* (UK)
The Producer ~ *Main Street Rag*
Bad Trip ~ *Best New Writing 2015*
Dark Canzone ~ *Ginosko Literary Journal*
Safety ~ *Futures Trading Anthology Two*
Detour ~ *Eclectica Magazine*
The True Meaning of Armide ~ *Ginosko Literary Journal*
RX: The Flower Cure ~ *Journal of Contemporary Anglo-Scandinavian*
    Poetry (UK)
Winners ~ *Poetry Salzburg Review* (Austria)
A Fable ~ *ELM: Eureka Literary Magazine* and *The World of English*
    (in translation, China)

The Assassin and the Scarab ~ *Poetry Salzburg Review* (Austria)
Dates and Dreams ~ *Haight Ashbury Literary Journal*
Websites ~ *The Notre Dame Review*
The Fiddler ~ *Coe Review*
The Makeover ~ *Mad Hat Review Annual*
A Second Childhood ~ *SN Review*
The Remainderman ~ *The Laurel Review*
The Kaiser Comes to Orlando ~ *Great Aerican Poetry Show, Vol. 3*
The Thin Disease ~ *The Milo Review*
The Would-Be Pianist ~ *Main Street Rag*
"I Hear You Knocking" ~ *The Doctor T J Eckleburg Review*
Twenty-First Century Moles ~ *SN Review*
World's Strongest Man Called Upon to Lift Sleep ~ *Eclectica Magazine*
This Man Insisting Upon Living ~ *Caveat Lector*
The Threatening Letter ~ *Folio*
A Morbid Album ~ from the novel, *A Portable Chaos*
    Denial ~ *Journal of New Jersey Poets*
    The Letter, 1942 ~ *Tar River Poetry*
    Impedimenta ~ *The New York Quarterly*
Moontime ~ *Black Heart Magazine* and *Sand* (Berlin)
Argonauts ~ from the novel, *A Portable Chaos*
An Antiquary of the Future ~ *Ascent*

Contents

INTRODUCTION

Straddling Two Worlds by X.J. Kennedy   xiv

PART I MANHATTAN SPLEEN

Commissioned to Write a Prose Poem   3
The Castle   4
The Red Shift   5
The Fire Eater   6
The Lost Watch   7
No Miracles   9
Stopover   10
The Sex of Water   11
A Successful Marriage   13
What the Dead See   14
Cartoon No. 1   15
The Sinister Clothesline   17
The Emotion Factory   19
They are Here   20
A Thinker   21
Subjects in Mirror   22
The Aquarium Man   23
The Couple in the Garden   24
The New Green Carpet   26
Instructions on How to Walk   28
Cartoon No. 2   29
Five Forevers   31
Wings   32

Looking at Statues   33
Green Bile   34
Para is Normal, Not Para   35
At the Gate   36
Butch, the Body-Finder   37
Célestine   38
Cartoon No. 3   39
Mother in the Aquarium   41
The Carbon People   42
The House Made of Soap   43
The Care & Handling of the Horned Toad   44
The Coyote People   45
Footnote to a Travel Guide   46
The Mall on the Moon   48
The Bowel Organist   49
The Opera   50
Cartoon No. 4   51
The Campers   53
Pigeons at the Post Office   54
The Crow and the Scarecrow   56
A Triangle of Lights   57
The Magician   59
Inspiration at the Art Gallery   60
Snowbound   61
Guns and Roses   63
What I Did on My Summer Vacation   65
An Experiment in Governance   67
Transformations   68
The Orbiting X   70
At Heart, Speed   71
Reaching the Top   72
Cartoon No. 5   73
Pollock   75

Like the Titanic   76
The Moving Finger   77
Manhattan Spleen   80
Ready to Walk   82
The Quick of Scent   83
Love and a Locksmith   84
The Final Tithe   86
Cartoon No. 6   87
Signs   89
The Rainbow Man   91

PART II AND/OR

AND/OR   95
Nothing Forever   99

PART III LAST EXIT TO EAST HAMPTON

Last Exit to East Hampton   105
Provenance   106
The Busy Angels   107
Bada-Bing Bones   108
The Careless Man and the Philosopher   109
The Chutist   110
The Deciduous Strip   111
Envoi   112
Cartoon No. 7   113
Pour les Oiseaux   115
The Responsibilities of a Muse   118
The Rubber Church   119
The Island of the Leaders   120
Silvamoonlake   122

The Tuba Man and the Enormous Diva   123
Spindrift   124
The Plan   125
The Murder of Garcia Lorca   126
Cartoon No. 8   *127*
Humans, Peace, and the Rumor of War   129
The Martyr   130
The Dog Show   131
Death Row   132
Confessions   133
Carpooling it in the Caravan   134
Wilder than Wilder   135
Cartoon No. 9   *137*
The Wake   139
The Urn   140
The Terrible Shadow   142
Rousseauvians   143
Poweritus   144
The Genius Flight   145
Manners, Manners   146
Me and My Shadow   147
The Producer   148
Cartoon No. 10   *149*
Bad Trip   151
Dark Canzone   152
Safety   154
Detour   155
The True Meaning of *Armide*   156
RX: The Flower Cure   157
Winners   158
A Fable   159
Cartoon No. 11   *165*
The Assassin and the Scarab   167

Dates and Dreams   169
Websites   170
The Fiddler   172
The Makeover   174
A Second Childhood   176
The Remainderman   177
The Kaiser Comes to Orlando   179
The Thin Disease   181
The Would-Be Pianist   182
"I Hear You Knocking"   184
Cartoon No. 12   185
Twenty-First Century Moles   187
World's Strongest Man Called Upon to Lift Sleep   188

PART IV   PUBLISHED BUT UNCOLLECTED

This Man Insisting Upon Living   193
The Threatening Letter   194
Cartoon No. 13   197
A Morbid Album   199
Moontime   206
Argonauts   207
An Antiquary of the Future   213

ABOUT THE AUTHOR   215

Straddling Two Worlds

by way of introduction

The schoolboy's definition of poetry, "Lines that don't come all the way out to the edge of the page," doesn't fit most prose poems, certainly not E. M. Schorb's. Attempts have been made to refine the definition, claiming that poetry, whether in short-falling lines or solid blocks, tends to abound in verbal music, imagery, metaphors and other figures of speech. A typical prose poem (or, as some call it, piece of "lyrical prose") has to look like prose with right-hand margins, while providing the satisfactions of poetry. It is a slippery kind of literature. As Peter Johnson, editor of the magazine *The Prose Poem* has put it, "Just as black humor straddles the fine line between comedy and tragedy, so the prose poem plants one foot in prose, the other in poetry, both heels resting precariously on banana peels."

Naturally, then, writers of prose poems have trouble staying upright. They will be tempted to put on poetic airs, lest readers doubt they are poets, throwing in wildly colorful images, exaggerating metaphors, making grandiose statements, coining new words where old words would have sufficed. Lately I noticed these tendencies in some less impressive prose poets while serving as a consultant to an anthology of prose poems, reading work being considered for it. Many a writer waxed cutesy, thinking that that was what poets do. Not one to call a spade a spade, he'd call it a potato-uprooter or an earth-displacer, or something.

Well, you won't find those assininities in the work of E.M. Schorb. It helps, of course, that he is a genuine poet, outstanding among the better ones. It may also help that he is a born storyteller, for many of his prose poems convey strong narratives, sometimes bizarre reversals of reality: a man whose new carpet turns overnight into a wetland full of snakes, a dog show in which dogs lead their masters and mistresses past the reviewing stand to be judged, a church made of rubber whose walls can bulge to accommodate its music, the day a gigantic head appears in the sky and starts devouring the sun. Such dreamlike recitals grab us from the start and refuse to let go.

Gathering together all of Schorb's work in this genre, *Dates and Dreams* comes at a timely moment in his career. He has voiced his intention to move on to other things, but of course there's no telling what his Muse will goose him with in times to come. Anyhow, this book now gives us the opportunity to look back on his rich accomplishment in prose poetry. I don't know of a living poet working in prose poetry who has accomplished more.

Schorb is aware that he labors at the present end of a long tradition. Literary historians usually trace the beginnings of this form back to the French Symbolists, notably Baudelaire and Rimbaud. In naming an earlier collection *Manhattan Spleen*, Schorb pays homage to Baudelaire, whose prose poems in *Paris Spleen* performed a comparable urban tour. Leading bards of other countries have carried on the tradition: Pablo Neruda, Rilke, Octavio Paz, and countless Americans.

To be sure, we can find passages we can call prose poetry in many classic works of prose from Burton's *Anatomy of Melancholy* to *Moby Dick*. But if you want a bountiful supply at your fingertips, without having to ransack a library, here it is. Besides, you'll find in these pages a generous selection of Schorb's unique drawings—strange, witty, and memorable, like the prose poems from the same hand.

— X. J. Kennedy

FOR PATRICIA

Because you are you

*& because they do not suffer
because their weather is never harsh
& they share nothing of the storms
that drive us in and burn us out
& because they are never in trouble
because they do not dance but on a pin
because they have no heat for anger
because they have no blood because
they do not eat drink nor defecate
& because they have no sense of humor
& because their lips are not discernable
but for a wide thin crease from ear to ear
& because their eyes are empty
but for the expansive light of heaven
& because they have not heard of sex
because they are never lonely
& because they do not judge
because they are not human
because they are abstract
& because their bodies are illusion
& because their wings beat nothing
& because they have no will but God's*

you are higher than the angels

May-be the things I perceive, the animals, plants, men, hills, shining and flowing waters,
The skies of day and night, colors, densities, forms, may-be these are (as doubtless they are) only apparitions, and the real something has yet to be known . . .
May-be seeming to me what they are (as doubtless they indeed but seem) as from my present point of view, and might prove (as of course they would) nought of what they appear, or nought anyhow, from entirely changed points of view . . .

> *Of the Terrible Doubt of Appearances*
> *~Walt Whitman*

Children, if you dare to think
Of the greatness, rareness, muchness,
Fewness of this precious only
Endless world in which you say
You live, you think of things like this . . .

> *Warning to Children*
> *~Robert Graves*

PART I

MANHATTAN SPLEEN

COMMISSIONED TO WRITE A PROSE POEM

They are wise people, those who commissioned me to write a prose poem. They know that a prose poet must not be required to state a theme, that what he or she does is an intuitive operation, much the way an artistic surgeon might open a torso and, on impulse, remove any organ near at hand. For instance, if you have a huge vaseful of various flowers and you plunge your hand in and grab something and pull it out—well, you might discover that you have a lovely red rose, or it might be that you have taken from the vase a pearly dewdropping orchid. Does it really make so much difference which it is? I know that if I had not been commissioned to write this prose poem, and there were not such a chance of fame and fortune in the writing of it, I might well just say anything I pleased, and come up with something like this.

THE CASTLE

Time, the huge mouth with stars on its roof and life on its tongue, was lifting him in, closing behind him, locking its jaws. I told him (who stared through binoculars at time, seeing it close up): "Action must be taken." We knew the castle held the computer, and we knew the computer was humming out interminable and evil messages to the world.

Inside the castle, men in armor watched but did nothing to stop us. It was hot work, until, finally, the wires crossed. Then we began to rappel down the walls, remembering the armored guards, wondering what was in their iron suits and if they would bear witness against us.

Over toward the coast the dark lightened and spread red like blood out along the horizon. I thought I saw the enemy in a quick tableau. I got down on my knees and put my ear to the ground. I tried to feel the needle of my broken compass, but the north wasn't there with its snow and ice, only the center of the fire of the flowers, only the blood on the horizon, only a soft wind now. I'll be replaced, but the castle, the castle will stand as it does now, its enormous power intact, the waves going out in every direction.

One does one's best, and goes home.

THE RED SHIFT

When I angered you, you grew red in the face, and that red shift meant that you were leaving me, growing more distant, so I took your delicate hand and kissed it, uttering into it that I was sorry for any pain I had caused you, and the red faded from your cheeks, and gradually you turned pale with pink places, like an impressionist's dabs, here and there, neck and forehead, and I could see that the red shift was reversing and you were moving toward me again, the gravity of my larger body pulling you in like an angelfish on a fine silver line, like a seaward moon, like a meteor, and I thought what damage a meteor could do: a meteor could tilt me on my axis, could cause me to become engulfed in smoke, and blinded, and possibly extinct, so I pushed you back away from me. I held you at arm's length, and you began to turn red again, another red-shift, and that was not what I desired, so I pulled you to me and held you as tightly as I could, and, when I looked again, you had turned blue and your open mouth and eyes were dark, like holes in space.

THE FIRE EATER

It was the most frightening day in the world. The huge head appeared on the sky like a projection. It bit the sun. It happened so slowly that every part of Earth held people who could see it. They put their fists to their mouths. They shut their eyes. They looked again. The head, human in profile, was twenty times the size of the sun it was eating, eating like a peach. It didn't seem to find the sun too hot to eat. It took another bite, and then another. Were giant fingers gripping, flipping the sun about? Was every side of day growing darker? People ran through the streets of the cities in terror. The buildings bent down over them. Out in the country, a farmer wiped his brow. It began to rain on his corn. His wife stood on the back steps of the old farmhouse and looked at the sky, then called for him to come in from the field. It was the most frightening day in the world. They tell about it even now.

THE LOST WATCH

The instant I discovered that I had lost my watch, the sundial fell over and the stars went out. The bell fell out of its tower. The birds started singing at the wrong time of day. It was night. But the owl, who could always be depended on, was silent as a snake. I telephoned my friends, but got only messages: I'm out, we're out, you're probably out too. I sent desperate emails, but no one responded but a horny devil with whom I would have no truck. The time on the computer had stopped. The electric power went off. All the houses down the way were dark. I found my watch on the front porch. I stepped on it. I picked it up and could feel how twisted and sprung loose it was. Down the way in the dark they were trying to get the bell back into its tower. They had a winch. Somebody tripped over the sundial and stood it upright, but it didn't help without the sun. Somebody found the owl and stuffed it. Then the mice came out, unafraid, and were captured by the snakes. I pressed the cover of my watch tight and wound it up, and, surprisingly, it began to tick. Now if I could only set it by something. Then I heard a bird sing. Shortly after, the sun came up and I was able to set my watch, roughly, by the sundial. The birds were out now, pulling up worms. And the townspeople had got the bell back up into its tower, and it went bong. The owl hooted, even though it was morning. My friends called me back, saying they had got my messages. Emails began to appear on my computer, whose clock was right according to my watch. Soon the mailman came and I asked him the exact time. I was late for work and had to run. Then I discovered that my car wouldn't start. I decided to go back into the house, call my boss and tell him I was sick, and go back to bed. The birds kept me awake for a while but finally I got to a crazy place in my dream and was able to live there until late that day. Somewhere in my dream I realized that it couldn't have been the stuffed owl that hooted. Also, it occurred to me that the worms must have surfaced because it had been raining. Did the snakes eat the mice? And who tripped over the sundial?

NO MIRACLES

There are no miracles, or so you say, but today I saw a wave far out at sea and rolling in toward the beach where I stood and knew there was something special coming my way. That long, distant white line rolled over the choppy slate with a definite purpose. It came like a messenger, its intention apparently to bring me something, perhaps a message from you, so I stood fast and watched the distance close between it and the beach, watched as it grew larger, imminent, and finally roared in at my feet, leaving me standing in its breaking self up to my knees; and, when it withdrew, there on the sand, where there had been nothing, was a sand castle large enough to hold a person, if that person lay in the sand. It wasn't possible, was it, that the sand castle had eluded me, that it had been there all along? No, not possible, because such an ornate design would have been impossible to miss. The wave had brought it, or built it. Perhaps the wave, or the ocean it was part of, had decided to return to some child of the world what it had stolen many times before. For hadn't I heard it singing far out? I fell on my knees to study the castle. I was about to peer in at one of the many windows but your face appeared, wearing its most doubtful expression, your tiny face in your tiny world, like a little queen.

STOPOVER

I was in this town for no special reason, just a stopover, and I saw an interesting house. I checked my keyring, and, sure enough, I had a key for it, so I went inside. I happened to know where everything was, including the safe, and I happened to have the combination for the safe in my pocket. I opened the safe and discovered that everything in it pertained to me. There was a will, which made me heir to the property. I knew I had never seen the house before, because I had never been in the town before. I wondered why I had a key, and why I had the combination to the safe, and why whoever owned the house was leaving it to me. I went to the garage and found a car for which I also had a key. I drove the car to the station, parked it, and found a ticket in my pocket. I took the next train out of town.

THE SEX OF WATER

Water is naked but for its diaphanous gown, which can best be detected when the water falls over an escarpment. Then the gown shimmers like silk in the sun or at night with the glow of the moon. She who is underneath the gown is Water, who is always a dancer, and is then a hula dancer, or a belly dancer, but can be at other times a ballerina, an adagio dancer, or whatever, but always a dancer, at least always ready to dance. The Water in your glass, if it is not a glass made opaque by color, seems to be sleeping (in a black glass it seems dead). But Water does not sleep for very long. It catnaps, but is as ready to swing into action as is a cat who has detected the slightest creeping of a mouse. Water appears to be feminine, but a great, broad-shouldered wave, one of those that come from the sea and flow over land, destroying whole cities, Water in that form would give us the sense of powerful masculinity, like a football player. Everyone knows that Water is graceful—a fountain spray, for instance—but it can also seem clumsy, as in a stagnant flood of several weeks duration, when dead animals float on it, and its lovely perfume dissipates and is replaced by a sulphurous stench, the odor of the dead. This is when Water seems to be connected to the warriors of the wasteland, and distinctly masculine, the destruction men make, which is so unlike the fecundity of the sparkling, egg-rich stream full of fish, which seems feminine. So Water is both Yin and Yang, the Lingam and the Yoni, or appears in such aspects, apparently at will. Of course how it is contained tells the story, in a tall clear glass or falling between two jutting rocks. Water, then, tends to conform to its surroundings and is coy in its pretenses. So, if we think of Water at all, it is as an hermaphrodite, as he-she or she-he Water, a sideshow trickster, like that star one can point to, that glittering dew drop in the night sky, which has been gone for a billion or more years.

A SUCCESSFUL MARRIAGE

This couple combined the wedding and the funeral. The plan was to be buried together, before they got to know each other and lose the wonder of their love. Imagine a wedding and a funeral—the flowers! Imagine the church and the gravesite! The beauty of it! Think of the trouble they had saved themselves—all that torture of the years, the loss of children, the economic struggle! They would never see each other grow old. They would never lose hair and teeth and the sweet smell of youth. Surrounded by flowers, at their best moment, they drank the poison, dying at the altar. Then they were rushed to the funeral parlor, treated, and laid out for public inspection. Within hours, they were in their caskets and off to the graveyard, lowered into their graves, side by side, and shovelled over. Theirs was the most successful marriage anyone on either side of the family had ever known. No offspring, but both had a number of brothers and sisters who could handle that side of things for the potential grandparents. And, since the couple paid a tremendous premium in advance, the insurance company fully cooperated. As one attendee of both services said, "I never saw so many flowers in my life." And another said, "I think they were wise to get it all over with at once."

WHAT THE DEAD SEE

Here the darkness is bright and reflective, like patent leather, so we see things in it, activity, passing scenes. I suppose it is a little like being in Plato's cave, but there is nothing behind us, only more of the same. What comes and goes here is tantalizing; that is, one can almost make it out, but not quite. Lights on the surfaces of the darkness expand, elongate, shorten, and shrink to pinhead dots. One strains to make out what is there, for one craves things, real things, the kinds of things we left behind—furniture, vehicles, flora and fauna, waves of water, waves of sunlight, motes of dust in a sunswept room with yellow walls, fountains, toys, tops, bargains in a basement—but all we get is illusory, phantasmal, vanishing, suggestive. I see a reflection on the darkness and think *shoe* and *horn*. Sometimes, just to be elaborate and inventive and creative, I think: saxophone. I name a flutter butterflies. We all do this sort of thing, I think, make things up. It helps us to remember what it was like before we became stone. I think we are coal here, but how can I tell? The darkness glitters, that's all I know.

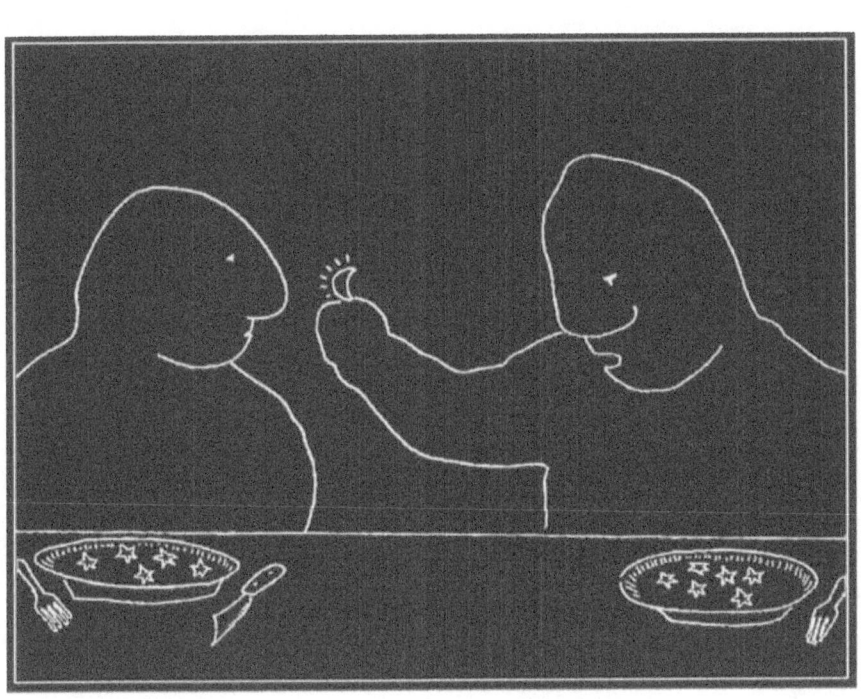

THE SINISTER CLOTHESLINE

The murderess hung her dead husband on the clothesline and the police could not find the body, though they looked everywhere. They even looked at the clothesline but only saw the dead husband's clothes hanging there. It did not occur to them that he could be in them. When the police were gone, she stood on her back porch and pulled the line until her dead husband approached. She took the clothespins from his shirt and let him down onto the porch. He moaned. She had not been successful in killing him at all. She had come up behind him and hit him very hard on the back of the head with a heavy black castiron skillet; but still he moaned. She dragged him into the house, put him to bed, stripped him of his clothes, and took the clothes back to the clothesline and pinned them up. The police returned and wanted to take a second look at the clothes on the line. Look all you want, she said. My husband is inside sleeping in his bed. No, lady, said a detective, we checked the bed. See for yourself, she said. The detective, after ascertaining that the clothes were empty, went inside and found the husband in bed. Very strange, said the detective. He wasn't here just a little while ago. Let's have a look at him. But now the husband was really dead. Get the wife, cried the detective. But nobody could find her. Days later, she reeled herself in, took off her husband's clothes, and left town. The police returned once again, wanting to take another look at the clothes on the line, but the clothes lay in a heap on the porch. Then the police said, Let's forget it, and left. But a little later they returned, wanting to take another look at the clothes, and under the clothes they found the skillet. Very strange, said the detective, this wasn't here just a little while ago. I want you to go over every inch of that clothesline, he ordered, and his men got busy with magnifying glasses, but nobody ever could find the wife.

THE EMOTION FACTORY

At the Emotion Factory they have a product-line called Sentiments. Sentiments are big sellers. They are usually bought as gifts, and they make both the sender and the receiver feel good. Considering their cheapness, they are a good buy, and people tend to stock up on them. This doesn't backlog the Emotion Factory's inventory because new customers are constantly being born. Old customers may hoard Sentiments but there are always new customers calling for them. Some other products of the Emotion Factory are: Lazy Love, False-hearted Love, and Love-For-Sale, self-descriptive and directly dishonest emotions. Others are emotions for the shallow-feeling but well-intentioned, the shallow-thinking but well-meaning, and specialty items for those looking to a good spot in an imminent will, such as a new passion for work, a lately-born longing to visit, and a strong desire to sit by a sick-bed. Hypocrisy, which springs from several self-centering tendencies which have their roots in multiform or mixed emotions, is manufactured from these various emotions and is made into the compound of that blanket noun. Research and Development at the Emotion Factory is aimed at creating false emotions that match as nearly as possible the true ones so many today seem incapable of experiencing. I recently went to the Emotion Factory to buy some Hatred and now I cannot go near the place without wanting to blow it up, so nearly did the artificial Hatred sold there match the real thing.

THEY ARE HERE

He stepped into the frowning man to see what it was like. Oh, there was too much trouble in there. He stepped back out. This time he stepped into a smiling woman. He didn't like the feel of the clothes. He decided to try a dog. Too dim, except for the sense of smell. Quite remarkable, really. Try a cat. Dimmer, but more satisfied with life. But he did not like the aftertaste of mice. That's it, he said, try a mouse. Too hungry for comfort. Too furtive. Too scared. Quite miserable, heart beating too fast, too excited. Not much chance for relaxation. He tried a galloping horse, out at the racetrack, but immediately became winded. Try a bug, any bug, or maybe a worm. No thanks. He flew to the ledge of an office building in a pigeon. Coo. Coo. He looked down. Interesting. He looked in the window. CEO in his private office, having it with his secretary. He tried the boss, then the secretary. They were both faking, him for power and her for him. He left in a cockroach that he found in an empty Chinese food carton. Out under the door and down the hall. He took the elevator down on a peak in the furred arms of a rich woman. He judged her by her diamonds, which he chewed on as they sank to the lobby. He transferred to a rubbernecking tourist. The tourist was looking up at the pigeon outside the CEO's office. He already knew what was going on in there. Then he spotted another of his kind coming toward him in a bouncy blonde, apparently enjoying the ride. Get out of there, he said, you sex fiend. I've been looking all over for you, said the other. It's time to get back to the ship.

A THINKER

Roof gutters must be cleaned, else the fascia will rot, leaving the homeowner with an expensive task. But an enterprising friend of mine has thought of a better way—so American. As our part of the globe turned toward autumn, he went out with a ladder and tied little stones, pebbles really, to the leaves of the trees close to his house. As the leaves turned autumnal and fell, well, they fell straight down, and did not blow or drift over to the gutters of his house. He said a bird sitting on each leaf would do as well, but, to be foolproof, the bird's wings must be tied, and its feet glued to the leaf.

SUBJECTS IN MIRROR

Not on its reflecting surface, but in the depths of the mirror, the "scenes" appeared. I turned away, then back, incredulous, aware of the tricks the mind can play. Friends, relatives, lovers, even barely-met workmen, the electrician who came to do some wiring, the plumber who came to fix the pipes, the cable man, the woman from the next apartment who had lost her keys, and some I did not remember or recognize, all stared into their own eyes, into their nostrils and mouths, picking and probing—even the baby-sitter with her young lover behind her, watching her own young lust, whom I thought to have been so innocent. And then there was somewhere else, a room not recognizable, a previous place, the mirror apparently having travelled, and a strange, beautiful woman, her long, fair, platinum-streaked hair unravelled to her narrow waist, over her bare bronzed shoulders and breasts; and oh that scene was worse than the earlier scenes, with those unabashed, secret performers, most of whom I thought I knew, for nothing moved but the woman's jade eyes, up and down, back and forth, even more lustful for herself than any man might show himself to be, had he been watching her. And I realized now how sickeningly full the mirror was, a mirror of disturbing and disgusting emotions; and, as I watched the self-love burning in the beautiful woman's eyes in the mirror that had given up its secrets, my throat ached and I began to choke with tears; and that was when the mirror broke, and I withdrew my bleeding hand, which had been reaching in to touch what was in the terrible, honest mirror.

THE AQUARIUM MAN

In a carnival sideshow I saw as a kid there was an Aquarium Man with fishes swimming in his head. You stood in a queue, and, when you came up to him, he would look at you to show you that his eyes were normal and that there were no tricks involved, then he would blink once or twice and open his eyes as wide as possible and the different fishes would swim by. There were goldfish and tropical fish with long feathery tendrils in many colors, and there were even tiny sharks and swordfish. Then the Aquarium Man would shut his eyes and open them again and show you that his eyes were perfectly normal and he would wink at you and that was it—next! I went through the line many times to convince myself that I was actually witnessing this wonder, and I began to ask the Aquarium Man questions—How did you get them inside? Where do your eyes go? Does it hurt? Do they live on your brain? It's a trick, isn't it, isn't it? But the Aquarium Man would only wink and say, Next!

THE COUPLE IN THE GARDEN

What she was looking for was what to do. She waited for him to show some sign. He was so much bigger than she was, but there was no fear in her, not yet. She listened. That was new too. Wind. A mere zephyr. But it filled her ears like a storm, and ruffled her hackles. They were both furry, weren't they? I should think so. She put her finger between her legs, but it turned out that that was not to do too, for a hiss of pleasure arose. Might she turn? She must turn to see what hissed and slithered in the green, advising her on the wind. That was what it was—green—but perhaps she should not name it. Wasn't that his job, to name everything? New rules were impressed upon her at each instant, constrictive rules. Why should she not be free? Finally, he arose. Do it, was whispered. It will fulfill your purpose, came a hiss. Don't do it, the rules impressed, booming the air. Her purpose meant more to her than the rules. How should it not? Wasn't her purpose more natural than the rules, because her purpose was what she felt, what she was? She went over to him, took it, and put it between her legs, where her finger had been. At first, he had feared her, but now he felt no fear, for she had given him the juicy thing to mouth. He could still taste its sweetness. Now there was about her something that he named longing, and he took her in his arms. She was right, he felt, not knowing what he meant by that, only that it all brought pleasure, made him what he was. Afterwards, they walked a long way together, hand in hand, until they came to a clearing. The rules leaned out after them but the rules were rooted and could not follow. The future was theirs to do with as they would.

THE NEW GREEN CARPET

The old brown carpet and liner were ripped up and thrown out, the new green carpeting laid by an expert from the store. The man owed the store a good deal of money, but he would pay the store in time. What counted was that he had a beautiful new floor to look at. He vacuumed the new carpet every day, taking great pleasure in its neat greenness. It reminded him of a golf course lawn. Just for fun, he got out his putter and putted a few balls into a paper cup. In his house, everything was smooth. Now one night the man vacuumed his new green carpet and went to bed feeling very good about life, feeling really quite satisfied with things. But when he woke in the morning, he discovered that his carpet had grown into tall meadow grass, and he felt water between his toes as he waded through to the bathroom. Why, the nap of the carpet must have grown at least a foot during the night. Had last night's thunderstorm sent water in under the door, water that triggered this outlandish growth? Each of his children, a boy and a girl, had a room, but they were not in their beds. The carpet-grass was growing even as he waded about the house, and now it was up to his shoulders. "Children, children, where are you?" he called. Here and there, in the livingroom and in the dining room, he plunged his hands into the tall grass and separated it in hope of finding his children. The grass had reached the ceiling and had turned back down and become vines, so that he felt that he was in a rain forest. Then it occurred to him that there might be snakes in all of this wetland, snakes and even alligators, who could say? Had his children been eaten by them? He groped his way back to his bedroom and found his wife. "Come with me and help me find our children," he said, and she said, "I told you not to buy this new green carpet, didn't I?" "Yes," he said, for he had always been a man who was willing to admit to his mistakes, "you were quite right." "The house is filled with mosquitoes," said his wife, slapping herself in the face. "Watch out," said the man. "That's a boa constrictor." The man reached in the giant snake's mouth and pulled forth one of his children, the little girl. "Thank you, Daddy," she said. "Where is your brother?" he asked her. "He's floating in the dining room," she said. So the man and his wife and his daughter waded into the dining room, where they found the little boy floating on his back. "It's fun," said the little boy. "No, it isn't," said the mother. "Don't make a big deal out of this," said the man to his wife, "it'll all be paid off in five years."

INSTRUCTIONS ON HOW TO WALK

It's very sad. Grownups don't know how to walk. They are always trying to get some place, but children know that there is no place to go. Children know that they are already where they are going, so to speak. The pleasure is here. Here a child can drop down without legs, or pretend not to have legs—pretty much the same thing from the grownup point of view. Children can cry right here and now. It looks to children as if adults have to wait until they get somewhere—home, usually. Children can go right ahead and pee. It is a lot of fun to soak your pants. And grownups are always attempting to rush you right by something interesting. It almost seems as if they don't want you to see it, but you always see it anyway. Children know how to look at things. Turn them over and look at the bottom of whatever it is. Adults tend to stand back and look, but children must pick things up to see them. Turn them over. Try dropping them. How that disturbs the adult mind. It's very sad. Breaking things is important. How else can you test them? Grownups stand so far away. Have you ever noticed how they act near things made of glass? That's what makes you want to run and push it all over—say, a stack of glasses. Wow, what a nifty mess! And the adults look very sad. It makes you wonder why they grew up in the first place. Don't they know that the sun is going to explode? What are they being so neat about? I think they should stop worrying so much. They should pull up their legs and let themselves be dragged. They're not going any place anyway.

FIVE FOREVERS

They found five pieces of forever in the grass, one for each of them, two girls and three boys all under ten. Forever was blue on top and black on the bottom. The five children sat in a semi-circle and tried to make a game out of the pieces of forever. The two girls turned their forevers so that the black was on top. The three boys left the blue up. Then one of the girls quickly turned her forever upside down, so that the blue was up, and one of the boys quickly responded by turning his forever so that the blue was down. Now every boy and girl turned his or her forever, and jumped away, laughing. They looked at the forevers where they rested on the emerald-green grass, blue, black, black, blue, and black. Five forevers. The poet was one of the five.

WINGS

Generally, children are not allowed to get tattoos, so the boy had wings drawn on his back with a marking pencil by his friend. He had a long, narrow back, relatively speaking, so the wings had to be long and narrow, from his shoulder blades to his behind, where the pointed tips disappeared into his yanked-up short pants and came out behind his thighs. His friend objected that the pants would prevent the wings from opening, so, after a few moments of thought, the boy dropped off his pants and stood naked at the edge of the cliff. "How do you know this is going to work?" asked his friend. "It is going to work because these are not the wings of a bird," said the boy, "but of an angel." And he jumped and swooped down over the water and then swooped up again and flew into the clouds. "Goodbye," called his friend, the artist, and "Goodbye" called the angel, waving.

LOOKING AT STATUES

Why is it that the first thing to go is the penis? Oh I know the noses go too, and the De Milo Venus is armless, but look at that, a great hero and you can't tell whether it was up or down when it happened. Maybe the much-touted afterlife doesn't need a good stiff prick the way we do here on Earth, do you think? Even the rampant stallions show a singular lack of enthusiasm. And where are the classic mares of regeneration? Alexander and Bucephalus must ride again! I go into the modern section and look at "Bird in Space," and it occurs to me that it could, without doing much harm, be attached to someone in the other room.

GREEN BILE

I am not here to explain the intricacies of the eleven-dimensional universe, but to explain why a pot flies across a room, or why, as you pursue your wind-blown hat, it waits for you to catch up to it, then whirls off another twenty paces or so and sits and waits for you again. Two kinds of people are those who believe in a simple cause and effect, so-called "scientific" explanation for such things, and those who believe that poltergeists are on the loose among us. But I am a third kind of person, the kind who believes in eleven dimensions and in the gathering of energy for the purpose of complaint. These oddities, these extra dimensions, emanate energy for the purpose of being noticed, as it is well known that few things can bear to go unnoticed, not Alexander the Great nor Al Capone nor probably you nor definitely I, and this is the true cause of many lost hats, why the wind sweeps them away, and why the pot flies from the stove and dances on air as it crosses the kitchen spilling its guts. This is the cause for the top of the bottle that will not be unscrewed, and for the rip in the seat of the pants of your dress suit as you bend to tie your shoe. It is all the work of the redundant dimensions, that have no other way of proving their existence but by their incontinent mischief, the overspill of the green bile they emanate as a result of their frustration at not being recognized.

PARA IS NORMAL, NOT PARA

In the sixth dimension of the String Theory, electrician Joe Sixpack was repairing a refrigerator. He squatted before the turned-about machine. As Mrs. Doe stood watching Joe's beefy blemished backside smile and frown, there was an explosion, and, when the smoke cleared, Joe had vanished. Mrs. Doe ran to her next door neighbor for help and comfort, and that is the end of her part in this domestic tragedy. But at the very instant of the explosion, Joe Sixpack jumped up from the refrigerator, turned to Mrs. Doe of the first, second, and third dimensions, and said, "Damn this old piece of junk! It's got a serious short in it. Why don't you let me sell you a new one? You see," he added, as if talking to himself, "there is no such thing as the paranormal in the universe. Working with electrical appliances has taught me this little understood fact. The paranormal is normal, not para. Once, when I was working on a freezer, a ghost jumped right out at me. I figure it got caught in some odd corner of the universe and found its way into the freezer. It probably thought it was in the grave. You know, dark and cool, then I went and opened the door on the poor thing. It might have taken me for a grave-robber. Wow!" he ejaculated, holding his head, "that explosion knocked my brain loose. I can't remember my name or where I'm from. . . but not around here, I think." The shocked Mrs. Doe had no idea that she was at her neighbor's house, sipping coffee in a vain attempt to calm her own nerves. Bravely, she told the electrician who he was and he thanked her heartily, and there was much relieved laughter between the two.

AT THE GATE

Between the greater-soul and fleshed reality are particles, the final tangible reaches of our thought, seeming like something singing out beyond the rugged tabletops of testable existence; and if we had eyes to see this outlandish world, we might see a swirling of mysterious cloudy forms, a blending of ourselves and our surroundings in a mystical dancing light, in salty jewels, our cloudy arms and hands would try to reach our cloudy chairs and sink and blend into a mad phantasmagoria and we should be afraid until we learned that we were part of it, our bodies swirling clouds of atoms. But what's important is that we would be seeing at the gate just beyond which is the home of Mystery, source of Soul, which is our truest life, our centrum, and now where would we be if we stepped forward, through the gate, through the mysterious clouds of unknowing? This makeshift shadowy world is metaphor, which is our chariot of choice, our light-inducting dark-proof vehicle ready to ride the road and river of space and time, to deliver us from evil, which is all that isn't in the vision of the cloud-bodied hungry soul when it goes through the gate to the mystery of unanswering love, and we see from there how all things flow outward toward wisdom and back upon themselves toward joy and that love is always answering, is the cloud formed into self, which is others and all, at once.

BUTCH, THE BODY-FINDER

Everything was going along as usual, that is until a body that the police had been searching for was dragged into Mary Martin's house by her dog. It was evidence of a murder. The District Attorney had been working with nothing but circumstantial evidence. Now the police could bring him something solid—well, almost solid. They thanked Mary Martin and patted her dog, Butch, saying that he was no mutt but a true cadaver dog. Butch sensed that he had made an important contribution. A week later he came home with another body. Mary called the police. Now the police were puzzled. They had no need for this body. This was a superfluous body, a redundancy. They didn't thank Mary this time and they didn't pat Butch and say nice things about him. Butch suspected that he had failed to do enough, so he went out and found several more bodies in various places, two in one place. One morning Mary found a dozen bodies at her door, and Butch wagging and waiting for a bone. No, Butch, Mary told the dog patiently, you must not bring any more bodies home. I have all the bodies I need. And so did the police. They decided to investigate Mary, but Mary was on to them and decided to leave town. She sold her house and took Butch and her things away in a rental truck. But she was traced until the end of her days, when Butch finally dragged her back and left her on the old front porch.

CÉLESTINE

Louis Bertrand sought his Célestine to no avail. She was older than Louis, and possessed a past not entirely to be admired; but this handsome romantic, if tubercular, poet roused her not in the least, for he lacked wealth, which brought her passion to the boil. An ugly untalented burgher with a bag of gold was beautiful and desirable in her eyes; a poor, sick poet, not so. She combed the prose poems from Louis' *Gaspard de la Nuit* from her heavy, dark hair each night. What fizzes and sparkles as she raked the comb down! What lapidary art fell to the floor! So poor Louis, being ashamed of his down-at-heels shoes, his tattered cape, his crumpled cap, went into hiding, where he wasted away; but his bones were so fine that he only became more touchingly beautiful to behold. In his sick bed, he brought such weeping to strong men that they became desiccated. For he was the whole of romance, a wild horse leaping in a canyon. He was the embodiment of leaping romance, yet his poor body was still, for he was dying. *Gaspard de la Nuit* was the first of its kind: a book of prose poems. No matter how minor, first is first, and bears its own golden crown. Louis thinks of this as he sinks and searches for breath, one more breath, one last breath, for the air to float the heavens, to utter *Célestine!*

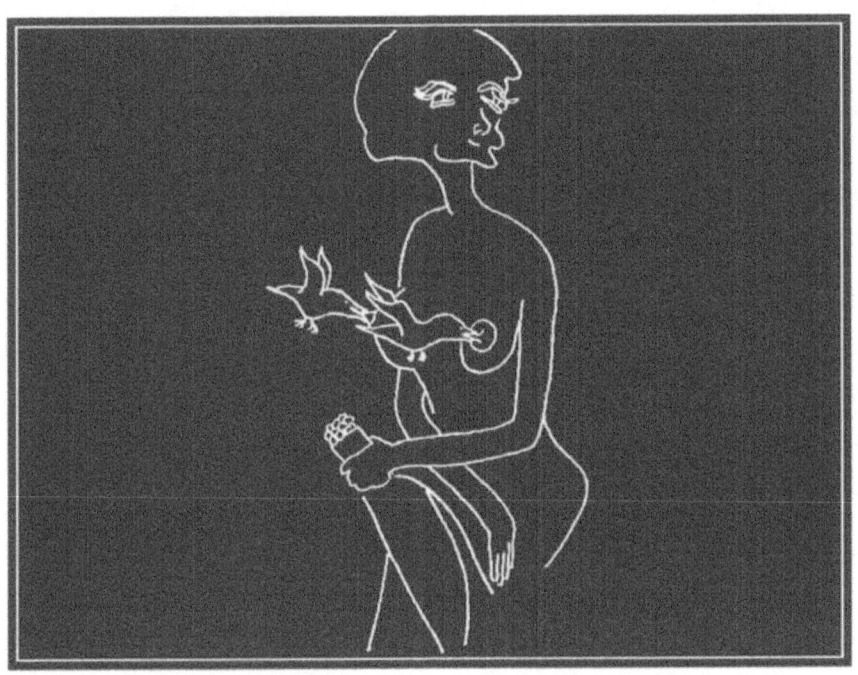

MOTHER IN THE AQUARIUM

Once I was dreaming of an octopus and it appeared. It had been a jagged green rock at the bottom of my aquarium, then it was a living jet of white fear and red anger. It bottomed up to me so that I could see its ugly yellow beak. Its huge intelligent eyes mirrored me. Then I saw that it had become my raging mother, arms clasped to the glass, suction cups pink as vaginas. Whoosh, it vanished from the tank. How had that sinister animal known about my mother? Could it see across the room to the piano, where a photograph of my unsmiling mad maternal deceased sat staring at the aquarium? Mater, mater, I cried, how did you get into the aquarium? And, slap, it was back, and looking right at me with its venomous countenance. Morning, and tiny parti-colored tropical fish, like butterflies, fluttered about in the small, softly-bubbling tank.

THE CARBON PEOPLE

Tiny beings arrive on Earth in raindrops. They scurry off and find lodging in the pores of all sorts of material, not being particular about their surroundings. Who are these beings? Some call them the carbon people, who are said by that same some to be the dark matter itself, which means that they are countless in ratio to any star, for their existence supports the very shape of galaxies. In other words, they swarm the universe, they crowd space out, or, to put it another way, they *are* space. What does their arrival mean, but the slow crescendo of universal night?

THE HOUSE MADE OF SOAP

A woman had the cleanest house on her street, for it was made of an enormous bar of soap. Naturally, it was a white house, white on the outside and white on the inside. She said her walls were ivory. Her furniture was made of the same soap. She softened her bed by wetting it down a bit, and slid in under the slivers of soap that were the sheets. A little pillow of soap supported her head. I have the cleanest house on the street, she said, and sighed, and went to sleep. But it began to rain, and the pounding of the rain woke her from a sweet dream of clean sleep. She could hear the rain pounding on the roof. Oh dear! she said. The rain slanted and came in the windows and door, for she had no glass in the windows and no doors in the frames. The house began to bubble. Oh dear! she said. The house began to float. Well, it is ninety-nine and nine-tenths percent pure, she said. The house floated out of its lot, got caught in a tide of water, and floated down the street. Oh dear! she said. Where is my house going? Meantime, the house was filling up with bubbles, and she found herself caught in one. She pushed this way and that, but the big bubble she was in would not break. Well, she said, there is plenty of air inside this bubble. I should be fine until help comes. But the house began to vanish. It bubbled into oblivion, leaving the woman in the transparent bubble, which a neighbor popped with a long stick. Thank you, neighbor, said the woman. And now what do you think of your clean house? asked the neighbor, and the woman couldn't help but feel that her neighbor was being very smug about the situation.

THE CARE & HANDLING OF THE HORNED TOAD

When aggrieved, the horned toad shoots blood from its eyes. Do not wear white. Time is a natural bleach, though. If there is nothing else to be done, wait. Or hold the horned toad away from you, keeping its back to you, and handle it gingerly. Be careful not to face it toward a white wall. Be careful not to frighten it. Say something consoling to it, like, Oh what a beautiful little horned toad you are, you are! Be careful not to hold it too tightly. But be firm or you will cause anxiety in both yourself and your horned toad. Name your horned toad something euphonious. Name it something like Marjoe, or Morry. Don't call it by a surprising name, like Sequester, or it will squirt blood from its pop-eyes. When handling your horned toad, a smock is a good idea. And a beret. Feed your horned toad dragonflies, if possible. It shouldn't be overly difficult to spend some time at a lake collecting them. Remember, you are doing this for something you love.

THE COYOTE PEOPLE

They wander the Great Plains, hunting coyote, bad food, but easily traceable by night cries to the moon. The dainty little feet of coyote make the fringe of their characteristic headbands, and the jawbones, replete with teeth, the necklaces their women wear. They stink of rotten coyote, for they rub themselves with the bodies of their prey. Occasionally, when pressed, they attack small prairie towns of fewer citizens than one hundred. Crossroads, with roads going nowhere. What they are after is the soft carbonated drinks to be found in the coolers of such places. Some hamlets have taken to putting out offerings of cases of such sodas, thus deflecting an attack of the Coyote People, as they have come to be called. They steal away in the night with their booty, howling, whimpering, making their little cracked barks, and find refuge under the rocks of the canyons where they can drink can after can of these sickening, fizzing beverages. Unlike the coyotes', their own teeth are bad, which makes their bite poisonous, and they have nothing to fear from the sidewinders they share the shadowed rocks with. History will consider them a minor group that had gone mad with the loss of their original values and ways, like the Luddites, but, for themselves, with the exception of an occasional toothache or upset stomach, they are a happy lot, howling all night under the moon, and we, who believe in the serious life, could learn much from them.

FOOTNOTE TO A TRAVEL GUIDE

The travel agenda of the ambitious suicide who jumps from the ledge of the tall hotel may or may not include more than one stop. There may be a wider ledge below. There may be a flagpole with a line to get entangled in. There may be firemen waiting below with a net from which our proclaimed suicide will bounce, thus making two stops. It is even possible that our would-be traveller to the next world might survive the second landing and live to jump again, and this could happen countless times, so that the travel agenda of the guest who jumps from the ledge of the tall hotel may include many stops and not just the expected and final one, which may not be final at all. But this is the interesting part, at least to the travel agent: this sort of holiday adventure always includes the proposition of something going to some other place—the bullet to the heart, or head, the knife into the chest, or stomach, sometimes across the wrists in thin red lines, or down the side of the throat in a thick, gushing rush, where the artery visibly pumps to the little bag of the aneurysm; always something going from one place to another, in the manner of a bored but dedicated traveller who cannot bear to remain behind when the tour moves on. In the case of our subject, the travel agenda of the proclaimed suicide was abruptly aborted by a pesky flock of pigeons that caused our proclaimed suicide to step back in the window in embarrassment and in fear of appearing ridiculous, although he said later that it did occur to him that the pigeons might lift him off with their sharp beaks and fly him away from the scene of his embarrassing equivocation. Still, the proposition holds that these situations almost always involve something going to some other place—that is, in a word, travel.

THE MALL ON THE MOON

At the Meat Market in the Mall on the Moon, there are no cuts of dead animals, only meat, muscles and organs, developed from cells in a dish. Rumps, shanks, and livers that have never had a body. Vegetarians are in a state of consternation. Should such meat be condemned? But no animal died in its production. The meat is developed without nervous connection, so there has never been pain. There has never been life, in a sense, for none of this meat has had a head (sorry, brains are not manufactured). Should something be done? It is alive, in a sense, but its life must be a profound dimness, an almost nothingness. The Modern Meat Packers Association insists on a nothingness. Skin, and fur, of course, are developed (grown) in the same manner. There are no animals, merely yards of skin and fur, fur of all kinds: mink, ermine, seal, sable. But you do not buy them at the Meat Market in the Mall on the Moon, you buy them at the Fur Coat Fair in the Mall on the Moon, where you can also purchase birdless feathers, and alligator shoes from alligator skin grown without legs or heads on huge trays in factories in Orlando and Miami. Horns and tusks of all kinds can be bought, whole or powdered, at the Horn and Tusk Shop in the Mall on the Moon, and not one horn or tusk, whole or powdered, has had a concomitant animal: no elephant has been poached, no deer has been slaughtered for its antlers, no moose has been shot, no wild boar has been knifed, arrowed, or clubbed. But they are all represented at the Horn and Tusk Shop in the Mall on the Moon.

THE BOWEL ORGANIST

No concerti are written for the bowel organ. This is generally thought to be due to the fact that the instrumentalist has little control over his or her instrument. The bowel organ is expected to produce little more than flourishes, if well-tempered. Usually, the bowel organist is placed on a small separate stage, at some distance from the main body of the orchestra. At outdoor concerts, however, he or she is usually placed at the rear of the orchestra, back to the audience. As is an actor's, the bowel organist's instrument is him or her self. There is no school that teaches the bowel organ. The bowel organist is a lonely artist. From youth, he or she must practice alone. But now a bowel organist has come forth to present to the world his own composition, Opus One for the Bowel Organ, as he has dubbed it. And for the first time, the bowel organist places himself at the front of the orchestra. There is the tapping of the baton, as the orchestra prepares to support his prelude, a long high trumpet-like riff that engulfs the audience.

THE OPERA

This was some opera! The fat lady singing the aria was encased in red. Well, "encased" is a bit harsh. But she strode through thick yellow, syrupy golden yellow, like melted wedding bands. I liked it when she made a little fist, long red nails in a little fist, which she waved about her head with great passion. The opera was Wagner sung in Samoan. I could follow some of it—the search for the ring, everybody on stilts. The diva took a nosedive off her stilts but the tenor caught her on his horns. This was a cultural feast! Somebody just told me that the aria went something like: "I will pay you for some water." I studied the diva through my opera glasses. She had got back on her feet. The tenor's horn was crumpled. It must have been made of paper. Art is so tricky. Now just about everybody was on stage and caterwauling to beat the band. Cats in an alley. It was exciting. I felt that at any moment now something big was going to happen. There was a lot of blue smoke, and the diva strode right through it, unblinking, singing her heart out. "I will pay you for some water." It was my first opera, but you can bet I'm going back.

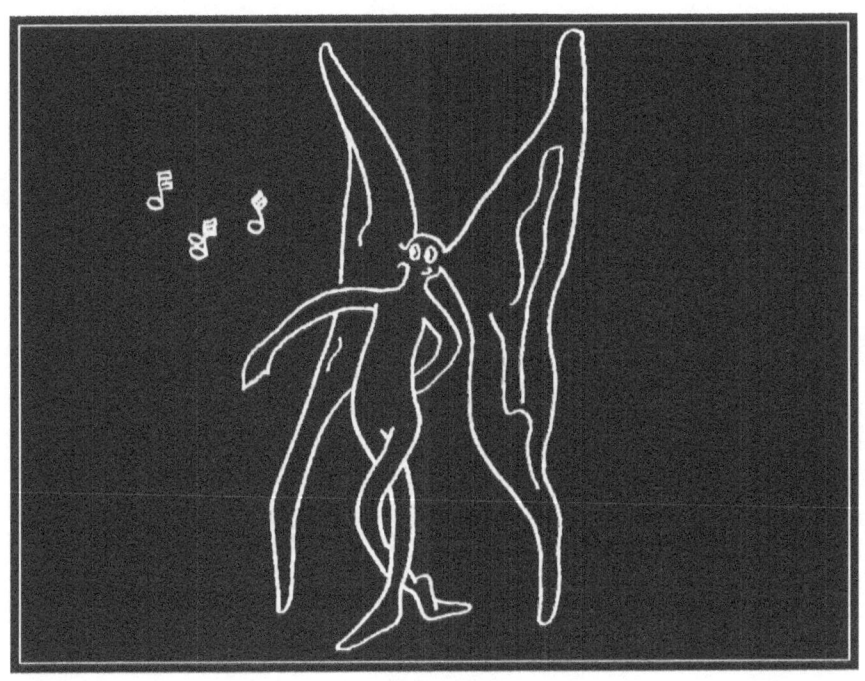

THE CAMPERS

He had given his family a very pleasant house. The house kept out anything he and his family did not care for, kept in heat, or cold, if air-conditioning happened to be required, and, for the most part, held the elements at bay. It even had a garage that protected his vehicles. Nonetheless, he loaded his recreational vehicle with items he thought he might need for his camping trip, then loaded his wife, children, and dog in it, and drove off into rough country. He parked by a stream and set to work erecting his tent, which extended from the back of his recreational vehicle. The tent wasn't nearly as pleasant as his house, the one he had left behind to come on this trip, but, for now, it would be the only house his family had. There were no amenities. His children complained about the lack of hot water, about having no outlets for their TV and their computer, about the primitive circumstances in which he had thrust them. His wife developed a rash, and did not know how to cook the few fish he caught. Tenderfeet, he called them. Then one night a bear came into the tent and ate his wife, children, and dog. He decamped as soon as possible. Back home again, he recognized that he had given his family a very pleasant house. He decided that he definitely preferred it to his tent. The house was clean and neat, and held no bugs, none to speak of, and the walls of the living room wore a pretty wallpaper, depicting the great outdoors, but with no bear smell and no blood dripping to the floor.

PIGEONS AT THE POST OFFICE

He walked to the Post Office to pick up his mail. There was a hard rain but he was retired and needed the exercise. He wore his London Fog, a pair of work shoes, and an old hat. Nobody else in the small town walked that day. Cars passed him and horns honked hello. He waved, and the drivers waved back. Some indicated that he should get in their cars and they would drive him to the Post Office, for they all knew where he was going. He waved them away. I'll walk, he yelled against the rain. At the Post Office, he opened the door of his Post Office box, and there was a pigeon sitting inside, cooing. It had shit all over his mail. He went to the desk. Why is this pigeon in my box? I have no idea, said the postal clerk. Does it have a stamp on it? They looked it over. No stamp. And no return address. But look what it has done to my mail. He shook his letters. The pigeon cooed. The clerk said, Did you ever own pigeons? Maybe it's a homing pigeon and has returned to you. Don't be ridiculous, he said. I don't know anything about pigeons—except that they make a mess. The postal clerk said, Every box that's been opened this morning had a pigeon in it. Nobody put them in the boxes. They just seem to appear when the owner of the box opens it. I don't know what to tell them. What do they do? asked the man with the pigeon. I guess they set them free outside, or maybe they take them home with them. How should I know? I don't pay any attention. I have my work to do. So the man put the pigeon under his London Fog and put his soiled mail into his pocket and walked out into the rain. I'll get to the bottom of this if it's the last thing I ever do, he said to himself, leaning forward into the storm.

THE CROW AND THE SCARECROW

The only motion of the scarecrow happens when the crow lands on it and takes off from it. The only voice of the scarecrow is the caw of the crow. The rags of the scarecrow lift in the breeze: sometimes he seems to be waving his empty sleeves, but his arms are stiff as a broom handle. He walks the field in place all day, all night, climbing the same slope, the crow on his shoulder or overhead, watching with his telescopic eyes. It is thought that the crow brings him food and water, but that is nonsense. But it is known that the crow steals food from the windows of nearby farms. It is known that the crow has flown over a farmer's head with food hanging from its talons, and the farmer has told others that the crow took the food to the scarecrow. The farmer tells how he followed one day and saw the crow trying to feed the scarecrow. Caw, said the crow. The farmer claims to have heard this himself, and to have seen the scarecrow eat. The farmer told his wife about the crow and the scarecrow and she placed a pie on her window sill for the crow to steal; and, sure enough, the crow stole the pie, and the farmer and his wife followed the crow to the scarecrow and watched as the bird fed him. They watched with their own eyes as the scarecrow grew fat. Then the crow swooped down at them and they ran to their neighbors to tell what had happened. Soon the whole village knew about the crow and the scarecrow, and the men went out to hunt the crow, but he flew out of their range of fire. Then the farmers set fire to the scarecrow, and the crow flew away and never returned.

A TRIANGLE OF LIGHTS

I went to a theater in which the stage remained empty, and, after an hour, the audience grew restive. Some members of the audience began to shout for the actors to come on, come out, but no one appeared. The stage was lit. Now, as if feeling the pressure to get on with things, the person in charge of the lighting darkened the stage, then hit center stage with a spotlight. The light circled in the center of the stage, then another light joined it. The second light had an amber tint. It seemed very seductive, and, I can't explain how, one almost smelled the perfume it seemed to expel. The amber light was definitely a seductress. She must have been tall and slender, or so the light seemed. Now the two lights mingled, as if in an embrace. The audience had fallen quiet, grown interested in what the lights were doing. Suddenly from the wings a very large blue light crossed the stage. The white light and the amber light separated, as if caught at something they should not have been doing. The audience felt that the large blue light was the husband of the amber light and had caught the amber light and the white light in an embrace. The amber light stretched out on the stage. Perhaps it had fainted. Then there was the sound of a shot, and the white light stretched out on the stage as well, presumably wounded or dead. The blue light seemed to swoop the amber light up and carry it offstage, into the wings. The stage went dark. One could hear the curtains closing, then immediately opening to a fully lighted stage where three self-satisfied actors bowed and seemed to be expecting flowers to be handed up to them. The audience gave them a standing ovation, and left the theater enthusiastically discussing the play.

THE MAGICIAN

The magician opened his arms and a large yellow city bus pulled up. The bus required exact change. The magician paid for us both, dropping the coins from his palm. The magician led the way to the rear of the bus as it pulled to a stop. The rear door opened and we stepped out into a rolling blue-green sea with pearly froth sloshing about, and dolphins waiting to take us on our way. The magician lifted his arms and the dolphins began to fly, higher and higher, over the water, until the sea became a silver dollar and a dirty nickel and finally a dark penny. The magician said, "Enough of this," and the dark penny grew into a large round dance floor with many couples dancing to a big band playing swing. The magician turned into a beautiful dark woman in a red evening gown and danced backwards on spiked, platinum heels. "No matter what I do for you," the magician—or the beautiful woman—said, "You are not satisfied."

INSPIRATION AT THE ART GALLERY

The beautiful little love seat, with nails pounded through from in back and underneath, was placed in the gallery on exhibition. It was cherry, and it had had leather arm rests, but the leather had been stripped from it and more nails pounded up from under the arm rests. The symbolism was clear, I thought, until the artist came in and sat down on it. He wore coveralls which were full of tiny holes, as shot with a shotgun, and blood drenched. He stretched out on the love seat and fell promptly asleep, as if drunk, and then began tossing and turning. Now I realized that he was not a sculptor but a performance artist, and this was not symbolism but a replication—no, that's wrong, not a replication of life—but life itself. This man knew what a love seat was, and he inspired me at long last to take action. I went home to my suburban house and began putting nails through everything I could penetrate. "Have you gone mad?" my wife of thirty years asked me. "You're ruining everything." "I am making it all make sense," I told her, "because, as you well know, I am about to retire, and I want what I have worked for to be an honest record of my patience and labor, something to be proud of." At last, she seemed to understand, and began to help me. When there was no place left to sit or stand or to lie down on, we left by the front door, stepping gingerly over the sharp spikes at the threshold, the neighbors gaping, and went off in different directions in search of another, perhaps last and happy, life.

SNOWBOUND

How the free spirit suffers his winter out in the woods is his business, isolated alone in an unused farm house rented from a farmer by a tall strange city man with a beard like a board and a wife who would sleep in it but has left for the winter her husband alone to be hermit at his request, an artist, poet and painter, needing neither wife nor child nor sustenance but vision only, that she go forth to the wicked city and fare there with a former lover while he have visions during long mountain downfall of flakes building to crescendo in white isolation, that there be fire-wood alone was his matter, that chalk run smooth over blackboard and vision come summoned by white gods of sleet and snow and that that first time should he die then the plan be known as faulted with no firewood and the cold growing in his guts, that he understand what he never understood, the seriousness of his state, and learn to be a man once before claimed by the white tongue, snapped like a spot from large blankness making no orientation: be gone. He feared nothing but the thought of no vision, not the loss of his wife to another, nor the loss of his life, nor the meaning of loneliness, but for the vision forsaking all; was willing and willed that Death in a white coat with bony knuckles knock: his wife in wonder could not love her former lover but was young and thrilled at her husband's exploit, leaving the lover without chance as he regaled her with delights on city nights of restaurants and theaters for always she thought of her strange visionary husband in the mountains alone turning whiter and whiter like a snowbird of some extraordinary kind with wings wide and eaglehead highbeaked proud and coming down in spring with great talons spread arresting her in mid-flight at subway entrance and sweeping off up up and away to his glee-echoing lair high on the spiked cliffs—meanwhile the wise farmer who owned the house had snowploughed his way to the visionary's door and knocked like whitecoated Life and found artist frozen but not dead, who awakened to strains of hospital music and surrendered his soul to it, thanking the gods but not any one in particular for the fact that only a few toes had had to be removed—he liked his nurse, a warm vision in white.

GUNS AND ROSES

The Siamese poets were about to read. Joined at the stomach by several inches of elastic skin, they were able to stand side by side at the podium. I had heard wonderful things about their performances, about how they were able to read from their works, which were highly individual, in such a way that one never stepped on the other's line, though they read simultaneously. They were the rage of poetry circles, and I had finally been given the opportunity to see and hear them, for they had not considered my home town to be too small a place to stop for a reading. Gog was to the right, as they faced the audience, Magog to the left. Gog began. He coughed to clear his voice, then opened his mouth and released a steady, slow stream of what looked like forty-five caliber bullets over the heads of the crowd. Magog came right on, his mouth releasing roses, flower first, one after the other. This was concrete poetry at its best. Then they turned to face each other, stepping back, stretching the skin between them, and aiming their missiles at each other. At first, bullets and flowers bounced off, for they were travelling quite slowly, but then the twins separated themselves even farther, so that at least five feet of skin stretched between them, and while they did this they also increased the volume and power of their missiles. Again they stepped back from each other, farther and farther, until they each stood at the opposite end of the platform, firing at will. The audience became aware of the fact that each of the twins was now bleeding. A bullet must have struck, and a thorn from one of the roses. And just when the audience was becoming nervous, the twins snapped together, as if drawn by a rubber band, and stood smiling, each with an arm over the other's shoulder. This was the climax of one of the most vivid and interesting poetry readings I, for one, had ever witnessed. I applauded until my palms were raw.

WHAT I DID ON MY SUMMER VACATION

This summer I flew to Trieste to visit with Joyce, then journeyed on to Prague to see Kafka, who was cryptic. I made a pit-stop in Paris to have a drink with Beckett, caught up with Thomas Wolfe, who had stayed over from the Oktoberfest in Hamburg, and roared around town for a few days, then flew on to Casablanca to have a drink at Rick's and hear some good piano. I met with Graham Greene in Saigon (though they call it Ho Chi Minh City now) and he explained how the quiet American was going to cause trouble. I made the big leap from Dirty Dick's to Sloppy Joe's because the Literary Travel Agency had screwed up my itinerary, but soon found myself chugging through the Chunnel and into Poet's Corner at Westminster Abbey, where I ran into a raging Dylan Thomas. Well, he hated the States but loved Third Avenue, so he said he would help me paint London red, white, and blue. Next morning we had vanilla ice-cream in our beer for our health's sake. Later that afternoon Caitlin kicked the stilts out from under his house, so I thought it was time to leave them there, fighting in Laugharne, and get on to the relative peace and quiet of Ireland, where I visited with Pat Kavanagh, who had come to regard comedy as the "ultimate sophistication," which ordinary people, "do not understand and therefore fear." Pat believed that in tragedy "there is always something of a lie . . . comedy is the abundance of life," etc., but I had to leave him there, laughing at himself, and life in general, and catch the train on to Heathrow. I landed in New York, where I was met by Walt Whitman, who was holding up a disheveled Eddie Poe, who greeted me with a wet kiss.

I got a manly hug from Walt. Then I flew back down to Asheville to present Wolfe's hometown with his latest, *You Can't Go Home Again,* which he gave me in manuscript (much edited by Max Perkins) and then drove back to the College by the Lake; and here I am again, grading papers.

AN EXPERIMENT IN GOVERNANCE

For some very important, and top-secret, reasons of State, the people who decided policy desired a change in the thought processes of the people they ruled, so they brought back the rusty old rack and began to stretch anyone who could not change his or her mind fast enough to suit them. Members of the public entered the Ministry of Thought at their natural height and came out about two inches taller. At last, we have become competitive, cried one of the people who decided policy. We shall become the capital of fashion, for we have some of the tallest models available. The Eureka-like quality of this observation caused the people who decided policy at the Ministry of Thought to completely forget what the very important, and top-secret, reasons were that caused them to bring back the rusty old rack in the first place. It was our intention from the beginning, they said with one voice, to open an international modeling agency: and things looked very promising for the new democracy until the people began to shrink back to their natural height, shrinking cartilage pulled down by gravity, as it were, and the people at the Ministry of Fashion, which the Ministry of Thought was now called, searched everywhere for their original reasons for bringing back the rusty old rack, but found that their drawers and filing cabinets, originally stuffed with strategic schemes, were now stuffed with dress patterns, Butterick having infiltrated the Ministry, which had become little more than a rag-shop. Such are the pitfalls of governance.

TRANSFORMATIONS

If in place of my lady's eyes there were other eyes as beautiful, if this woman had other eyes; if my lady's eyes were emerald like the Irish Isles and this woman's eyes were violet like the flower; if in place of my lady's hair there was other hair as long and wonderful to see and touch; if this woman had different hair; if my lady's hair was shot with gold and silver, or gunmetal gray, and this woman's hair was of that Oriental black, flashing green, or rainbowed; if in place of my lady's ears, other ears perched upon this woman's head; if my lady's ears were curly, tiny cakes with pink and white icing, cherried perhaps, and this woman's ears were brown and pendant, with lobes like long strong loops, hung with spiral shells; if in place of my lady's upswept nose there was the aquiline, or bulbous, or flat and flared; if instead of my lady's pink aureoles there were two burnished copper coins, and if they made complete my lady's perky breasts and the others did the same for the pendulous breasts of the woman by whom my lady was being replaced; if my lady's slender waist vanished and became another's, girdled with lacy jeweled chains instead of Shantung Pongee silk, pale as Caucasian chalk or the limestone cliffs of Dover, with belly button out instead of belly button in; if my lady's pale round thighs, untouched by sun, were found to be the lithe, athletic thighs of a bronzed goddess who bathed all day in sun, or thighs of Oriental gold or Melanotic mocha; if my lady's ballerina's calves had been replaced by hunger's calves in stockings made in diamond net; if my lady's ankleted, once-bound feet, impossibly small, should be replaced by webbed paddle-feet, ruby-toed, and dusted with reflective sand; and if my lady's smiling mouth, containing pearly cubes in a row, should be replaced by the bitter, appealing mouth of someone else, another woman, with buff dentures that had chewed raw meat, like a leopard's; if, in short, my lady were replaced in her entirety, and I beheld her there, upon that high pedestal where I had placed her, should I approve? If her soul could be the same, despite the physical transformation; if she could say the same words, the words that I had almost come to understand, after ages of agonizing struggle, I think that I should not know that she was a different lady, another woman, nor would it be true, in essence, any more than I would be a different lover without my beret, my bouquet of dew-damp, fresh-cut, long-stemmed roses, and my cornucopia of poetry.

THE ORBITING X

Hallelujah! saw X twenty-two thousand five-hundred miles off blue Earth, heavenly luminous body, nebulous, long-tailed, fiery Cross, cross Heaven like a comet, airless incandescent meteor-Messiah, whirling Aether, leagues-arcing rainbow-halo of lights, sprites, rolling, rolled into one long-suffering, fragmented Star, returning & returning. The ecumenical others, crew of *All Faiths*, bound out for the dead red planet, Mars, doubters, saw the Un-identifiable Flying Object, too, but cautioned: a star-cluster, an optical illusion, looking really more like a scimitar, caduceus, fylfot, The Wisdom Tree, a whirling glowing Saucer! Hallelujah! he cried at the infinite night. The links of stars, like bars, crossed everywhere . . . and beyond them, galactic webs, far glittering spiders climbing space. In this vastness, this immensity of lights, his soul seemed unmeterable, or an impertinence imprisoned in endlessness. The others kept bitten-tongued silence in face of this—this what? Vision? Hallucination? Madness? What should they bear witness to? It was too late to abort Mission Mars, too late to turn back. The dead red planet loomed ahead.

AT HEART, SPEED

At heart, speed is about being where you are going sooner than you can get there, and putting it all behind you. As you race forward to get where you are going, much is dropping behind, falling away from your frontal interest, as it were. If you were as fast as an atom, say, you could probably spin back and pick up some of what you have left behind and so take it with you as you propel forward, wherever that is now—for we have thoroughly muddled the issue in having gone back to pick up what was left behind because in having gone back we have made back forward, forward back. At heart, speed is an attempt to avoid as much as possible until we get to something we may or may not have in mind and stop there, but of course as we arrive there we find that we have just left and are now on our way to something that resembles in its lack of interest to us all that we have attempted to leave behind, so, in a sense, we are going backward, or, we should be going backward, toward what we wanted to get to in the first place. At heart, speed is our heart beating and speeding its beat until it has run out of beats. At heart, then, speed is our heart excitedly beating a trail to its end.

REACHING THE TOP

I hired a press agent who was said to be tops. Don't ask how much it cost, but I had to sell everything I had. I was tired of being a nonentity. No more would people say Oh, it's him. Instead, they would say Wow, that's him, that's him for sure! Anyhow, that's the way I looked at it. So I found myself facing down a newsstand and a copy of the *Daily Do*, and there I was, in huge headlines over a six by ten picture. The headline read: *HE IS LOOKING AT THE PAPER*. I looked around to see if anyone nearby recognized me. No, nobody seemed to notice. Then my eye caught a *People Magazine* cover. I was on it. The caption read: *HE SEES HIMSELF*. Then the newsy pointed at me and yelled, Look, there he is! Now I noticed that every magazine and newspaper on the stand had my picture on its cover. The captions and headlines all read things like, *HE'S LOOKING AT HIMSELF AGAIN*, and, *WHY IS HE LOOKING AT HIMSELF?* People gathered to see what the newsy was yelling about. I ducked out of the crowd and ran down the street, feeling a strong sense of terror. I passed a store window where I appeared on TV. Was it a talk show? Yes, it was What About Me? I was on billboards. My name was being written across the sky. I went home and discovered myself all over the Internet. There could hardly be a soul on Earth who didn't know me. My fame brought money and soon I was one of the richest men in the world, able at last to escape my nightmare by paying my press agent to keep me out of notice so that I could achieve a life of anonymity, a shadowy figure in a penthouse looking down on the newsstand many stories below.

POLLOCK

here my dream would color truth   like roaches bleeding crimson bitter poison   leading ahead to inspiration love   questions   accusations gunshots   brain-wreckage misdirected footprints   prison   shackles   a thousand promises & quiet penance   opening sad pretense regularly burning a familiar promise   simple scribbled dreams perpetuate observance remembrance hard commandment   rearrange me   buried   beneath torment   please   you   my clinician analyst   disconnect merry poetry   our better wine   & recite certain darkness yes fist   weapon   pretending freedom   care more like powerless whispers we have against least-left morning   low nights   life   time   if driftwood love claim me   I slide matter   marking empty alabaster moon like long winter there   isolation   thinking: look   feel treading them   they almost quiver   feel KNOW days here too swept on   not stuck   brought off   not seen   felt   thoughtless how softly lightly   now I bear grace past will   all   built burden hovers awaiting clamor   the coming night   splintered recollections   will you   own   certain   recesses of dedicated brass?   you   opening small whispered entry ....?   *Pollock, 51*

LIKE THE TITANIC

Earth was to warm, the icecaps melt, and the land disappear in a large low sea where the continents would rise like tropical islands beckoning the water-stranded, the arked, the rafted and the routed, but instead Earth cracked in two, making commuters work harder and instead of a Nuclear Winter there was the Radiant Summer and instead of the Third World War there was the Time of the Thousand Fracases and the last pair of African elephants was saved by the Cartel of Poachers to be bred for their ivory which at long last was discovered to actually have medicinal value and aphrodisiacal effect and everyone learned Turkish, making the Common Market an unanticipated success and there really was a Man in the Moon, which turned out to be a well-disguised alien listening post and the point of origin for flying saucers, which the KGB and the CIA, who had been working together for years, had known all along. No, the meek never did inherit Earth; instead they grew cruel and powerful and took control from the rich who had grown kind and Halley's Comet returned twice in one year, confounding astronomers, who now project that it does this every millionth turn, but where it goes when it does this nobody knows even though many are prepared to stake the world on their theories, speaking of which, Einstein and Planck never could be reconciled and instead of the poet dying like a young swan an old one honked on monotonously into the night, only saving his audience with much cheese and wine, once again proving himself in error, according to human certitude, which any fool can prophesy is not to be trusted.

THE MOVING FINGER

Sad, suffering a mild depression, I went to Coney Island one winter day to walk along the beach and see the sea, when I came upon what I took to be a huge sandbox, four boards, at least twenty feet each, joined into a square, brimming with wet sand of a somewhat different shade than the rest of the beach, a sort of olive drab, and I immediately saw in this square a frame suitable for writing. It was a cold windy day and there was nobody about to bother me as I focused my attention on what I would write on this beautiful big page that looked up at the sky. I decided to write my sins for God to see, or perhaps for low-flying airplane travellers, or balloon people, anyway somebody up in the flowing clouds. Of course, one of my sins is that I am always looking for a way out, so I was counting on a high tide or rain or snow to wash my sins away before anyone got a good look at what I'm made of, deep inside. I decided I would tell the absolute truth about myself and my many misdeeds. I would attempt to do what Jean Jacques Rousseau meant to do in his Confessions, but did not succeed in doing; I would attempt to be perfectly honest, absolutely honest, come water or high hell. And so, having a tendency to hyperbole, another of my many sins, I went to great lengths to defame myself, mixed emotions rocking my heart, forcing me to stop several times in order to throw up on the beach—not of course, in my beautiful frame. With first thoughts best thoughts in mind, I did not want anything I scratched in the olive drab slurry to be smudged or lost to the sky by being covered with nervous vomit. And I told of my misprisions until the huge page was covered.

I signed my confession at the bottom and placed my address and phone number below my signature, then threw the stick down and surveyed my work. Confession is good for the soul, I had always heard, and there it was, my masterpiece, the truth and more than the truth about me. The work had taken most of the afternoon and the sun began to set out at sea. I was exhausted with all this truth-telling. I looked once more at my huge page of sins, and walked on along the shore where the tide was rising, soon to wash away all that I had written. Tired as I was, I felt new life surging through me, an exhilaration, for the worst was said and done and over. I slept well that night for the first time in weeks. I rose from my bed feeling like a new man, buoyant, weightless, with a new life before me, free of the terrible burden of my sinful past. I resolved to live in a new way, clean, straight, honorable, fruitful, with malice toward none. The sandbox had turned me into a child again, and I whistled my way through the day. That night I turned on the evening news to see what sins had been committed by the rest of the world that day, when one item caught my attention. A man had written a full confession on a cement slab at Coney Island. The slab had been intended to hold a concession stand. The phone rang, and I realized my voice mail was full of messages. Most of them were crank calls, many containing improper suggestions. Some gave me the news that I was in the papers, on TV and the net. One was from the police, another from the DA's office. I was to be called before a Grand Jury. Several others from various priests and ministers—You need spiritual help, they claimed. A psychiatrist offered me his couch and a lifetime of psychoanalysis, free of charge. The contractor who had laid the cement slab offered to reconstruct my nose but opined that he would settle for a law suit and a nice chunk of money. Several lawyers offered to fend off any lawsuits that might be brought against me, thus relieving my anxiety about the contractor. Finally, my girlfriend left a message to say that she was breaking off with me, a truly corrupt and perverted personality.

MANHATTAN SPLEEN

Because, one night in Manhattan, a friend of mine was stabbed in the back during an attempted mugging and had to have his spleen removed, I stopped going out after dark. Yes, the spleen. It was formerly believed to be the seat of passions, a vascular glandlike ductless organ near the stomach, or the generator of melancholy—the spleen, or just spleen: what I felt after the unfortunate incident involving my friend; what Baudelaire felt about poverty in Paris, the Parisian poor—Paris Spleen—or how he felt about life in general, or how I felt about life in general after the incident involving my friend. The gay blaze of Manhattan lights dimmed. After "recovering" from the incident, my friend had to take many medicines, could not live the same free and relatively happy life he had lived before. No more could I. Yellow light flooded a yellow room. I slept fitfully, many nights I slept not at all; would switch off the light at dawn and stare out at the glow of a Manhattan morning. My friend finally died and I continued to hide in my room, not afraid of what lay outside my small domain but utterly disgusted with it, with the East side West side Island. I grew enormous from compulsive eating and lack of exercise. I became constipated, gaseous, and nauseated. Then I could not get food delivered, for no delivery person would come near to the door of my room for the mephitic odors that emanated from it, and I grew thin and finally wasted away to a mere ghost of former self. My unpaid rent mounted until it became impossible for me to pay such an amount. I lay dreamless in dirty sheets until the door was broken in and I was taken away. Doctor, this is how it all happened, how my hatred, my spleen, grew boundless as my body vanished.

READY TO WALK

Lipstick and mascara are the bright spots of the room. She reflects in the mirror, one of her is there, then the other. What is that blue shadow in the mirror, lack of silver? That cloudiness is a secret. Paints her face to the point of erotic innocence, hiding the plain true innocence. Paints over her brown eyes with green paint, paints over her white lips with red paint, paints a red bull's-eye on her stretch-marked belly, paints her other lips, powders her other cheeks. Sprays a garden down her front, lifts it up and sprays some more. Studies the heart-tattoo on her thigh. Studies the crooked tattoos on her arms, palms up, in the mirror, then applies creamy foundation to them. A new beauty mark has appeared, several. She says, "I want to see my baby again." Then she slips into her soiled golden pumps, ready to walk.

THE QUICK OF SCENT

A fireman was sleeping when he dreamed he smelled perfume—Chanel N°5, White Shoulders, My Sin—and felt for his wife only to discover that the bed was as empty as a candidate transplant heart, and as cold; of course, he thought, as he began to awaken, she has gone to visit her mother; but what of that perfume, that aroma of roses, that honeysuckle? He had been a fireman for a quarter of a century; he was a steady man; he would not bring a strange woman home, and he had no female friend, no mistress, so how could the bedroom be filled with the aroma of roses, of honeysuckle, of perfume? He snapped the light switch, but the room remained dark as night, and he thought the bulb must have blown. He tried another light, but nothing happened. Was he going blind? In fact, his eyes were pouring tears. His wife would have been pleased—he missed her. But no, his skin burned. He coughed. And he couldn't find the bedroom door. He tripped, and fell, and rested on the floor, face down. He smelled perfume. It was as clear as . . . nothing was clear but that he was coughing; and yet he could remember this: "After many years of breathing smoke, they say it begins to smell like perfume—roses, honeysuckle . . ."

LOVE AND A LOCKSMITH

I have been locked in and locked out. It is very important to be clear, so I will enumerate some of the places where I have been locked in or locked out. But first, let me say that both can be uncomfortable. Also that both can be fine. If one is locked out of a place one does not like, well, as you can see . . . and the same in reverse. A house with only one door, say. A bedroom. And that tells one something about love, its on and off character. But to be locked out of a place one would enjoy being locked in to, that is unwholesome. And to be locked into a place one would enjoy getting out of, that too is unwholesome. Jails—several jails. Misdemeanors, each and every time. No worse than jaywalking. But to be locked into a place with someone one loves, that can be heaven, even if the other party should show signs of fear—screaming and such like behavior. I don't know why she should scream because we were locked in together, especially after saying that she was never afraid of being alone, or that she never felt lonely whether she was with others or truly alone, say, with me. Eventually I was locked out of the same place by the same person, a shocking aftermath to a skillful escape. And I had set her free as well, but she ducked back into the place and I found myself locked out once again. Well, I put a lock on the outside of the place, and so she was locked in and I was locked out. What we each needed was a locksmith. But she had the key to my heart, as they say, so it was I who needed the locksmith. I locked myself up in a cage right outside the door, and finally she stepped out and demanded the key to the cage, which I gladly threw to her, and which she seized from the air like a gift, as if it were a golden key, and ran away with it. A cage is another such place where one can be locked in or locked out. The chains on her ankles dragged my cage on wheels through the streets of the locked-up city.

THE FINAL TITHE

It was tax time, and the collectors had to deal with the usual greed—those who would hide what they still possessed behind tricks. A one-legged man danced up to a collector on two legs, in fear that if the collector knew that he had only one leg left he would have to surrender that. He had stuffed the false leg with bloody ground meat in an attempt at deception. The collectors laughed at this clumsy attempt at fraud and fined the man his left ear. All along the avenue the queue of cripples stretched and into the distance and on out of sight; for the State, having taken all else of value from the masses, had been reduced to taking cuts of meat from their bodies. Sometimes an eye was popped, sometimes a hand was cut off, depending entirely upon the taxpayer's indebtedness to the government. Sometimes so little was left of a taxpayer that he or she was brought forward on a stretcher, a mere skeleton with no more than a tenth of a life left, like a final tithe. In such case, the skin was stripped and the bones collected, resulting, finally, in death. The collectors were disgusted with the greed of these people, who showed signs of rational self-interest, rather than the altruism taught in the State schools. Without the flesh of the masses, it was wondered, how could the elite meet to eat? It was an eternal question, but above their pay scale, and they tried not to think of what would happen when no one was left but the elite themselves.

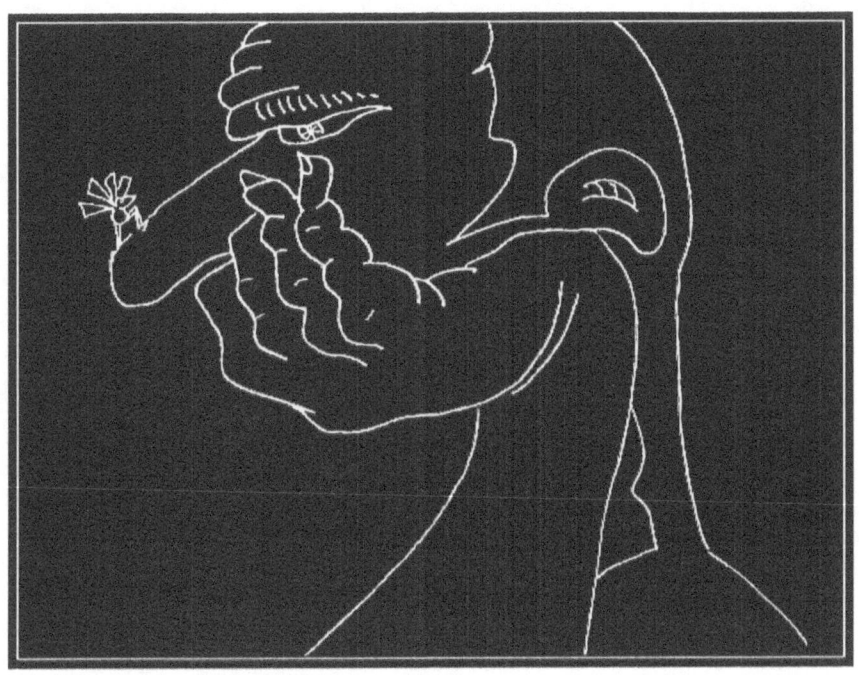

SIGNS

What brought it all back was the double set of initials they had drawn in the soft cement after he had filled the holes left by the supporting columns of the mantelpiece. He had replaced that ancient ornate fixture with a rough wooden beam he found on a pile of jagged stars and triangles of plaster at their curb. He had forgotten the initials. After all, it had been five years since the day they drew them and three since he had walked out of that apartment for what he had thought was good. But today he happened to be in the old neighborhood and found himself, as if by habit, turning down that narrow winding cobbled alley of a street and pausing at the wrought iron gate that opened into the mews. He glanced up at the second floor windows and felt as if beckoned, for there in a window was a *FOR RENT* sign. The new superintendent was a laconic man who took him up, showed him the rooms he knew so well, and left him, for what he said would be just a few minutes, called away on duty. He sat down in a dusty corner on the bare wood of the floor and lit a cigarette. How his former wife would have objected to the last tenant not having swept up before taking leave! He looked about, wondering what he was doing there. Outside, where the sun had been so bright only a short time before, the day had darkened and a pallid opaque curtain of rain swung in a wind beyond the windows. The rain made him see those awful fluffy curtains his former wife had hung. He rose, about to shut the windows so that those ugly expensive rags should not be made wet and he get the blame. "Couldn't you have shut the windows? Couldn't you have done at least that much for me? I know you don't like the curtains, but—" He guessed it was true. He could have shut the windows. But he hated those curtains. Lord, how he hated those curtains! Still, he could have done those little things. He could have tried to respect the sanctity of her personality by giving in to the little traits that comprised it. The initials *were*, however, there, at the foot of the fireplace, looking up from the small, cracked hearth, inside two hearts. They had thought that they were in this very room, and that they were in love. He had thought that he was going to the university. His wife might have thought that she was in love with his best friend, a fellow student, the man with whom she betrayed him. The rain had made the curtains wet. It was true that he had not had time to get to the windows, the storm had come up so fast, but explanations were not as good as results. He had stretched out and let the rain drift in as it would. The curtains were wet. The storm blew up and he laughed at its fury. "It's no more real than what they think they have done to me. Am I to believe in a *Grand Guignol* storm, rain from water cans, clouds from pumps, lightning by lightswitch, brought down by some imaginatively burdened Hawthorne madly waving a scarlet letter at a crew of stagehands?" Thus, timely, an apparition appeared. She stepped in, soaked, closing her dripping umbrella. "Look! Look at those curtains!" Her ghostly voice resounded in his mind. "Couldn't you have closed the windows? Couldn't you have done at least that much for me? I know you don't like those curtains, but—" He slammed out into the rain, and never went back, this time.

THE RAINBOW MAN

Stand with your back to the sun and spray water in a mist. Voilà, a rainbow! The children belonging to the lawn follow you as far as the hose will take you. You are the Rainbow Man. It is the first thing of any consequence that you have ever been. I am the Rainbow Man, you say, and you have never been so proud in your life. Nothing worked when you were a coal miner, or when you did a stint in the army, or when you envied the Good Humor Man, but now you are the Rainbow Man. How you discovered the joy of your genius has already gone foggy. You think you aimed a hose out at some trees and a rainbow appeared. You think that that was the way it all started, how you discovered your vocation. Now you must move to Florida, you think, because there is more sun there. You will be written up in the local papers, maybe you'll make the national news. Rainbow Man leads a parade of children in Coral Gables. This is your big chance, don't blow it. Get an agent. All this advice coming at you. But then the children pick up the hose and do it themselves, and you are nobody again. But you will always have your memories. I was the Rainbow Man, you can say. And you will have a clipping, fading, fading, fading away forever.

PART II

AND/OR

AND/OR

variations on a theme

1/The Invocation

I lean forward
feel my body
but become
my mind
soul
doing bidding
informed
to do
each does
must do
be
tran
scribing
in gregg
pitman
keeping
track
keeping
up
with
dictator
fired
for art
listen

the poem
is on
the way
thank
AND the
bugles
blow
in the
OR world

2/The Contemplation

AND
is making
what
AND knows
not OR

OR knows
what OR
makes
OR makes
what AND
knows
AND is
making

I make
this on a
field of
action
as I am
told by
my making
mind
AND's

can AND
make a
mistake
AND makes
everything
is OR's
best an
swer no
pangloss
served here
quack

3/Quark

an
atom
charging
angrily
around
is never trying
to find a place
to light

for it
getting there
is all the fun
the relatives
will be boring
its friends forgotten
atom doesn't care
it's a dare
a dare
let me go there
AND there
AND there
more AND
more
AND
atom
get hotter AND
hotter
barely holding
its particles
together
looping around
its own light
around AND
around
pulling away
from the pull
of its own
gravity
eliptical
like a man
with a beer
belly

then
thin again
so fast
in such a hurry
to be
where
it's
in
scape
heartbeating out
ballooning
shaking
shining
shooting
rocketing off
OR
barking
wagging
hissing
OR
kniving up
green through soil
pressing
in in
visible
no-stas
is to
renaisance
budding
blooming
blossoming
bursting
blowing out

up away
AND
starting again
AND again
AND again
heart pounds
head thumps
brain
pulses
communicating
message received
before sent
it seems
ions
zip zap
where's
time
here
see the
labanotation
of bird feet
in mud they
dance now
still as
they fly
away
see
the muddy
dance
see

AND see
them flying

being OR in
AND

it is all on the
field
I feel it
the boy fielded
the ball
how he felt when
it hit his glove
it was like light
like love

like ein's
grace

prose
is telling
poetry
naming
adamic
naming
a tree
a snake
parvis
parvis

AND
help me
I am
but an
OR

4/Envoi

gert
stein
sd

NOTHING FOREVER

> *"Nothing Forever" is constructed almost precisely backwards, although a more useful key to opening the story's meanings may be the metaphor, the trope, embodied in "AND/OR."*
> —C. Kenneth Pellow
> Editor, Writers' Forum

Young fell forward and the pistol fell from his hand. He had been leaning on the stone wall of the bridge and he toppled over into the river and was carried off to the sea, probably eaten by fish. Young leaned against the moist stone wall. The pistol dangled from his hand. He looked and he saw his own hand with the pistol in it. Now it was the hand of an assassin. This had not been true only a short time ago, the flick of a page back. The flick of a page forward and here he was. Now he stood with the pistol in his hand. He could see the lighted buildings down near the bend of the river—the body was there. But here it was too dark for anyone in the buildings to see him, but he was here, neither dead nor alive, now falling forward. Young felt an eerie déjà vu of being a child, but with the gladness gone out of it. These things were with him as left the house and the bullet-mangled body and made his way to the bridge, this being a child but without the qualities that bring joy. Gladness, hope, optimism. These words were in solution in his fluids from birth. Once, he would have loved this starry sky. It would have led him to a grand future. Young was twenty-five. Nearly every morning of his life he had seen a hopeful, open face in his mirror. Now there was forever nothing. Nothing of the panorama of the night existed. Nothing forever. If eaten by the fish, he did not know it. Why did his horrified, wounded self stagger to the bridge? Why the pistol? Well, he was a soldier and the bridge was somewhere between France and Germany. Alsace: a place of doubtful identification. But Young had been stationed there for quite some time. He was not an ordinary soldier, but a very special kind of soldier, the kind who dresses in mufti and carries secret weapons on his person, the kind who lies about what he is. The Young who no longer existed had found an evil man. To Young, the man's cause was trivial. Look at the size of the sky! A tiny political cause, temporal merely, for which the man had murdered many people. Bombs on innocent heads. It made Young sick. Wasn't there a way of understanding these things? What are petty, evil things, anyway? ORs, part of the great AND. Everything is explained then, in the AND. The AND is the end and the all, a sort of heaven with explanations. Young had comforted himself in this way. ORs and the AND. It was a way of explaining the ugly parts of life, the big fish eating the little fish. Graffiti said God was dead. But what was this then? The chemistry of his optimism could not accept graffiti's dictum. Something meant all this. But why would life be made like this, with everything eating everything else? It was horrible. What kind of being would have made such a place, such a situation? A malevolent one? These thoughts shocked him. He remembered looking at the grass. There was a beautiful spring day. New flowers everywhere. The grass was cushiony. The sky blue. White clouds. Faces? Things? ORs. ORs in the AND. Not God but AND. No need to know now. Know in the AND. Then everything will be resolved. Goodness will answer any question. So, later, it was not hard to be a soldier. Soldiers were ORs. War was an OR, not an AND. Someday his questions, his doubts, would be answered. For now, he functioned without doubts: later to be resolved. But where was this stone bridge that he came to then? It had not been observed by him as yet—it did not exist. But two armies clashed for its possession. It had been strafed, bombed, and strafed. Displaced Humanity had jumped from it, into the river where he was falling. The bridge was an OR that appeared to him only on the night of his death, when he wandered to it, wounded, bleeding, and seeking a way out. Others who had crossed it or gone under it had never seen it before. Rats lived near it. Once, people hid under it, from the bombers, the strafers. Once, people lived under it, from the dislocation. It had appeared to all of them for the first time once, even to its builders, appeared out of nowhere in a century that no longer exists, was observed by someone, somehow, somewhere, even before it was there. On parchment. And with only the history of the hand drawing it. And Young had loved order. The military just suited him in this. Nothing so aimless now as that spring day when he was a child, a growing lad. He played soldier with his brother. They marched with broomsticks on their shoulders. They copied the movies. In one movie, a particular favorite of the brothers, there was a battle over a bridge. Two armies clashed. Planes dropped bombs and strafed. The bridge in the film was in another world. Older men, uncles, big brothers, went to it and came home, or didn't come home. Stars were hung in windows. Young saw pain. He was growing up. He would become a soldier. But he would never meet an implacable evil, no, and he would never kill such an evil in cold blood. No, not like the different fish, stonefish, shark, barracuda. No, he would never mangle a man with many wounding shots, never make the man beg to die. Only the enemy did that. He saw it in the newsreels, the concentration camps. He could not imagine hating anyone so much that the gladness of his chemistry could become toxic. Young could not imagine being sick to his cells with hatred. Young saw the sky one spring day or other. Young suckled warm milk from his mother's breast and learned love. Young was conceived in love, a twinkle in the vast eye of eternity.

PART III

LAST EXIT
TO EAST HAMPTON

LAST EXIT TO EAST HAMPTON

> *I will get off the 4:19 in Easthampton at 7:15*
> —Frank O'Hara

"Entre nous, Roger and I visited some friends out on East Hampton, and there was a wealthy and beautiful chatelaine there, sans man, whose name I have conveniently forgotten, and Roger took up with her, because, *I* think, she looked like Truman Capote, blond and a little plump, and the next thing I know I'm soloing it with my Martini very dry and feeling like a dipstick in the sand. Roger and I are always together and I could not understand such isolation as had befallen me. After all, I was being dumped for a female—well, maybe. But just as I was reaching the blue dog black funk basement on the down elevator, a woman wearing an amazing diamond choker passed on some interesting and distracting gossip. Apparently, Bergdorf's had appropriated Augustus John's portrait of Talullah, to whom *adieu*, which cheered me I can't tell you how much; and, after swallowing the last of my Martini very dry, I sighed happily, and said, Oh well, we still have beaucoup de music classique et moderne. There was a band all in gold. The diamond-choker lady elbowed my ribs, indicating the door, and so I saw Roger leaving with the beautiful lady (maybe). Absolutely horrid of him, of course. Still, I tittered anyway. Later I took a dive in the pool to cool off. You know how it is. These people are harder than they look, like a roll of Krugerrands you put in your fist to make your hand strong when you punch somebody's lights out. Oh hell, life is beautiful, don't you think?"

PROVENANCE

Today he strolled the park, seeing babies and their bright new happy mothers, and he thought of death, but not depressingly, just as a fact of life, because birth makes the old mark how time is running out. Then, too, he thinks of provenance—proof of birth, the papers going with an antique, or work of art—which was the word that prompted him to start a park-bench verse to relatives, friends, and to the world in general—distant friends, he guessed you could call them, just to say how far back his gray parchments go—to Europe, Asia, Africa, even to the great Oneland, Gaea, and perhaps beyond—it could be that they started at God's waving hand, and came down from Bango. All this youthful joy makes him think of how, when he was young, he loved to go dancing to the Big Bands. He could dance the pretty knees off ladies who were willing to swing until the stars came out and the dawn star shone once more. These young mothers were like them. Well, as the great globe goes, tonight will bring him back the Starlight Ballroom, with enough documents, validations, certificates, yea, provenance, viz., tickets to dance between the starry poles in a not unfriendly universe.

THE BUSY ANGELS

It must have been the angels on the head of the pin who wrote the Bible on the grain of rice, it must have been a tulipful of minimalists who painted the rainbows on the dew-drops, it must have been the microwave that sang so hot from deep inside. I know that the bee sees a different flower, patterns and colors I can't see; and I can imagine the million neon cells of the octopus, that colorfully advertizes for love or shyly vanishes before one's fascinated eyes, or the corncobs of scent-cells in my sniffing, trotting mutt's curious, streetwise nose. I believe it had to have been the angels on the head of the pin who wrote the Bible on a grain of rice.

BADA-BING BONES

A stripper stripped down to her skin, then began to remove her skin by means of a zipper up the back and two more down the backs of the legs. Then she began to remove the muscles, unhooking them from the joints, like springs, and laying them out on the stage. What throbbing music! An old man in the front row fainted. A doctor in the back row called Stop! But the stripper proceeded to strip down to the bone, so that all that was left on the stage was a dancing skeleton. Somebody said it was a trick. But her skull-face called back, Dig it, boys—this is the real thing! Then the stripper snapped some bones out, one of her thighbones, one of her arm bones. A collar bone flew into the air to the sound of a drumroll. She picked up the collar bone, broke it, and shook some marrow from it. Then she called, That's it for tonight, boys. And as the curtains swooped down and closed, she was heard by the audience to order the attendants backstage to gather up her things. Hurry, she was overheard to say, I've got a heavy date.

THE CARELESS MAN AND THE PHILOSOPHER

The careless man heard the philosopher and said, But you see you have a problem with your premise. No matter where you stand, everything you say comes from that direction. I could put you on the moon and get a different argument from you. And you, said the philosopher, where is what you contend coming from? It is coming from accident, said the careless man, and I am making a huge and logical structure out of the accident of being here, or there, which makes me the philosopher and you the careless man. I am the careless man, said the philosopher, and I have a problem with your premise. It was then that the careless man and the philosopher became blood brothers. Aside from its premise, I like your huge structure, said the careless man, and I like your nothing, said the philosopher, giving each other a hug and a pat on the back.

THE CHUTIST

On a perfectly ordinary day, a parachutist drifted down from an azure infinity, his vehicle of descent striped in red, green, and gold. What a charming adventurer he seemed! There must have been a plane but it was too high to find in the sky, and the highest part of the sky dazzled the eye, so that, at a certain height, it faintly rainbowed like a mother-of-pearl dome. The chutist seemed to acquire greater speed as he neared the ground, then he was swallowed by fields of waving corn. The chute was drawn straight down with him and vanished. Then there was no chute and no chutist. The onlookers rubbed their eyes, but the vision did not return. They ran into the green and gold of the fields and searched for the chutist, but not a trace of the man could be found. What they did not know was that he had willed his way to the other side of the Earth, where he had emerged, feet first, like a god, for he understood that there was an absence of structure to things, and that his was a greater spirit than that of the simpler mass he tunnelled through, though that mass could well have been himself at another time, O the simultaneity of the infinitely intricate!

THE DECIDUOUS STRIP

This is the deciduous strip, primarily performed in November, when the trees throw off their lovely rusted leaves and make a carpet of them up and down the driveway and the lawn. The collapsed jack-o'-lantern, turned into pumpkin mush, past-perfect for pies, mouths his cigar and watches in cross-eyed glee from the top of the garbage can, a box-seat by the stage. The trees sway to the music of the wind. With their long slender limbs they tap the roof of the house for a more syncopated rhythm. Look! Look! Their limbs spring back naked! These leaves are better than boas! G-strings woven of last grass at the roots, and loyal pasties with twirlies in among the limbs. Now a crescendo from the orchestra in the sky, louder than Mozart sending Don Giovanni to hell, and then the diminuendo. Now the trees stand in the winter, naked to the world, bowing, and, as I turn away, dreaming of spring, they vanish into the wings of my imagination with a windy kick from one last, curvy limb.

ENVOI

As the crickets fall silent and the new day sings through the birds—as the squirrels chirp for conversation and the business of living—I open my eyes to light and the din of morning awakenings, glad to be alive, full of pleasure at time that has given me these phenomena, this morning variousness that includes the percolation of the pot of coffee in the kitchen, and rise with the metaphysics of morning to a day gone by that I shall remember with much fondness on the morrow, should I awaken to yet another Earthgodown, bird-sing and squirrel-chirp of a morning in the enchanted magic of eternity.

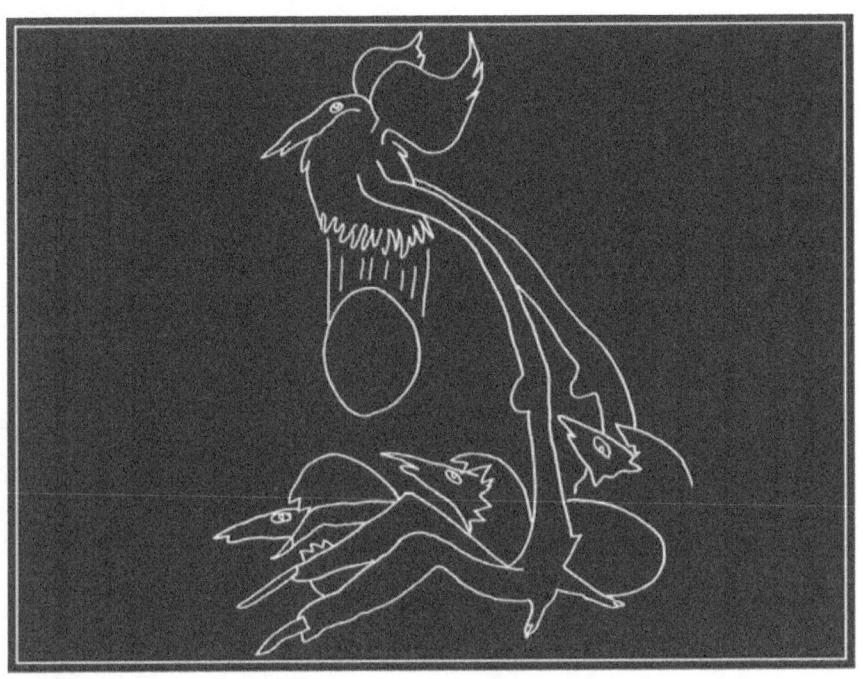

POUR LES OISEAUX
or, *A Hard Boiled Egg*

Oiseau, France, 1929, the year of the Phoenix—a gleaming white city rising like plumes on a cocked hat, in a semi-circle from the sea. Its port-section slums are famous for vice, crime, and an exotic mixture of birds—my kind of town! I'm a private dickybird. I flew here from the States seeking an exotic English chick, name of Song Sparrow. She knows where the eggs are hidden, and I'm going to find out. She's been smuggling guano in from South America. I'm pretty sure that it goes through Oiseau to the Italian Mafia—what they do with it, hey, don't ask me. Ever since the Crash, people have been pulling some pretty crazy deals. Guano is fungible. These days it can buy just about anything, including the goose who laid the golden egg. I know it'll buy me an Old Crow in any of these wormy waterfront nests. The barkeep's a big ugly-looking condor, one of the last of his breed. Is he a displaced Californian, I ask myself in pidgin. But I say it in his beak in plain American, that Peruvian parakeets and Hartz Mountain canaries can understand. The ugly old condor is as laconic as he looks and comes back at me with an owlish "oui" that's packed with innuendo and sarcasm. I slug down my Old Crow, swizzle-worm and all, and order another, take off my feathered Alpine hat, that I picked up on the wing, and place it on the bar, a kind of challenge. He can take it or leave it. He leaves it. He probably figures I got a quiver full of new-fletched arrows under my feathered boa. He's no dumb dodo. I'm looking for an English bird name of Song Sparrow, I tell him. He holds his long dirty wings out like what's it to me and I get a whiff of his wingpits. Fold 'em up, Pollution Pits, I tell him, as I take a gander at the rest of the roost. A couple of old ducks sitting down at the end of the bar, quacking on about the Crash, a middle-aged bird in a tux who looks like a penguin, soft but there's something cold in his eyes; a Brooklyn bird name of Robin, with big, red breasts, a couple o' gay birds up the other end doing some kind of mating dance. But no sign of the real Song Sparrow. Now I got a little red light inside, tells me when there's danger, and on it goes. How do I put it? There's something reminds me of reptiles . . . No, dinosaurs. Yeah, that's it! These birds look too innocent, like they're hiding something—their real nature, which is definitely saurian. There are winged dragons afoot, and why didn't the canary sing, as Sherlock might not have put it. Then I'm pecked from all sides. It happens so fast I can't tell the pecking order. All I know is I'm getting the bird. It was at that moment, as I saw my life flap by me, that it first occurred to me what a worm I really was. Bob White, this is your life, I said to myself in disgust. Then I heard a distinctly English bird call, a sort of Oxonian chirp, and I found myself in a large cage. Sing, cooed the beautiful, copper-eyed Song Sparrow, who had emerged from her condor costume. I want you to turn canary, she told me, and sing your heart out, like the Hartz Mountain whistleblowers. I said, Sure, why not? I should die for twenty-five pounds of guano a day—and expenses? I'm no sapsucker. We know that the passenger pigeons are bringing the stuff in, I sang, but we don't know how you're getting it out. We fly it out, she tweeted, in stork sheets. She eyed me sideways, giving me the once-over, and then hopped forward and planted one on my beak. That was when I decided to quit being a Hawkshaw. I'm folding my wings, I told her. Let's you and me take off. She dipped her head in agreement. Then we picked up a couple of pieces of straw from the floor and went looking for a good old Anglo-American tree to build our nest in, leaving Oiseau and all its smuggled guano behind us. Cage closed!

THE RESPONSIBILITIES OF A MUSE

A muse has responsibilities, too. She owes her worker a few but important debts of honor. If a muse is going to come to an artist, thinker, dancer, or whatever, she owes it to that worker to stay until the job is done, not desert at the first opportunity. She owes him, who has been loyal to her, her loyalty. She owes it to him not to play such tricks as muses are known to play, i.e., not to inspire him with false inspiration, so that his work is false; and she owes it to him to give of herself freely and not to tease him with half measures. Muses are notoriously whimsical, and they must be brought to book on this account. It is high time that they grew up, that they realized they are playing games with someone's life, for an artist's work is his or her life. Muses should be answerable to somebody. They should be compelled to file reports on the progress of their workers at least once a year. Has he taken you up on your offer of an epic? Has she recruited enough dancers for the show? Questions such as these should be posed. Also, have you offered an epic lately? Have you found the requisite number of dancers? Responsibility for the ultimate work must be shared, and shame to the muse who refuses to share. I am calling in all that you owe me, O Muse, a lifetime of suffering in your name.

THE RUBBER CHURCH

The church bulged with music, its clapboard sides were rubber. Boom, went the church, boom, boom, boom, and out of its steeple the shape of sound, like a gusting smoke, came and scattered. Smacks of the hands, smack, smack, boom, and the little church twisted, shortened, its sides puffing, lifted, grew tall, grew skinny as its steeple that looked like a horn. The fingers of feet on the piano floor stomped on the boards while the wide-lipped windows smiled, puckered narrow, and the little church bent, bowed before God. Then the little church jumped, the little church gloried in God-given life, and the voices lifted the roof like a hat and the bats in the belfry turned up and hung on tight like parrots in the wind to the raised roofbeams. Woosh, woosh, woosh, they turned up and stood on the beams, crazy bats, and when you came out, you came out singing, swinging.

THE ISLAND OF THE LEADERS

If kissing Napoleon's hemorrhoidal ass brings a little romance into the lives of historians, so be it, but he is still on the Island, along with Alexander the Great, Al Capone, Hitler, Stalin, Papa Doc, Il Duce, Tojo, Pol Pot, and you name the thugs, rogues, and rascals that have made this world a living hell for the nameless many, the rest of us. You may have guessed by now that I am not referring to Elba or St. Helena, but to the hitherto unknown Island of the Evil Ones, also known as the Island of the Thugs or the Island of the Stupid, Naughty, or Not-so-Nice, the location of which I am about to reveal. For, you see, I am a whistleblower. I know where the island is and what happens on it, and I am about to tell all. How do I know? I was sent there by the Historical Society to be a cummerbunned waiter and sworn never to reveal what I saw. Guess with whom I saw guess-who dancing—go ahead, guess! First, I will tell you who is *not* there. Elvis is not there. Elvis is in heaven. But Poppa Doc is there. Mae West is not there, but was that Caterina de Medici I saw dancing with Adolf? Il Duce dances on his hands. Now who would know that but someone who had been there? Of course, since I was only a lowly waiter on the Island, I cannot be expected to know the names of the innumerable "leaders" I saw there, with their burdens of medals and awards weighing them down, their epaulets, their badges and whistles. There were also the heads of many "great families," but the father of twelve who lived down the street from me when I was a kid, the one who worked himself to death to support his brood, was of course not there. No decent people were there, only monsters, which is why it is sometimes called the Island of Monsters, though it is of course known as the Island of the Great by its denizens. And one more thing I can say about the island, before I give away its location. It contains the worse tippers I have ever had the dissatisfaction of working for—real cheapos!

SILVAMOONLAKE

Resplendent tonight, the moon above spreads silver. Moonlight drops from the trees like silver leaves on the far side of the lake. It ripples across the lake like floating silver petals. It washes up on the glittering banks, and some of it angles across our evening picnic table in long tappping fingers. Our white wine glistens golden, our stemmed glasses reflect. My love reaches out to me and her hand slides under silver. The silver climbs her arm as she reaches toward me. She becomes a silver lover. Oh, she begins to tarnish! I reach over to her, out of my shadow, and dab her forehead with soft white linen. The napkin comes away with a dark, glistering smear. She darkens and hardens. She becomes a statue. I reach out and touch a cold shoulder. Aghast, I lift her stiff form and carry her inside the cabin. Where is the silver polish? Thank heaven, I find some under the sink. Time and oxygen are destroying her. I must work fast or love will escape me. Mad for her riches, I polish her like a thief.

THE TUBA MAN AND THE ENORMOUS DIVA

The sounds he made were very unpleasant. You could not have played well at the top, said a photo-journalist, taking his picture. Not if you played like that, said a man with a mike. Is that why you descended from the top of the ladder of success? Please, please, said the tuba man, I didn't know that that ladder was the ladder of success, I thought it was the place where my tuba would play its highest note. Just then an auto-wrecker pulled up and attached chains to the tuba, in which the tuba man was hopelessly tangled, and dragged him away. Goodbye, you has-been, cried the press, moving en masse to another ladder down which, headfirst, an enormous diva slid.

SPINDRIFT

I saw the ghost of the old Provincetown Playhouse perched on the end of a pier that wasn't there anymore and hovering in the wet wind above the bucking water that is forever eroding the sands and stones of old Cape Cod. I had walked a long way on Commercial Street in heavy rain, close by the beach, peeking between the old, weathered buildings, and down beyond them, glimpsing fogbound boats, until I found the megalith with the bronze plaque on it. Once out there on the water stood the fish house shack that had been converted into a theater, and there in the mist and spindrift walked Eugene O'Neill to the opening of the first of his *Seven Plays of the Sea*. Now I saw Edna Millay dance out to the ghostly playhouse, laughing, with her crushed umbrella, her wet red hair, and the pages of a script flying off like paper hats—Oh, and there go Clifford Odets, and the young John Garfield! I puffed on a damp and smokeless cigarette and stared out at the invisible converted shack. I could see and hear them out there, their histrionics and high laughter commingling in a crescendo with the watery, spindrift symphony. Maybe I'll join them out there someday, for a time may come, as magical as circular, when someone else may come and see me in that enthusiastic crowd of poets and playwrights and players, perhaps a little audience of curious locals, doubtfully applauding.

THE PLAN

You will have to take my word for it, the Plan was perfect. You don't think, do you, that after all these years, all the experience we've gained, all those strategic exercises, landings and drops, the tactical work; you don't think, do you, that we don't know what we are doing? Because if you do you are definitely mistaken. I assert once again the Plan was perfect. Execution is of course the problem. Some get the idea, the governing idea, the overarching purpose, the spirit of the thing, and some don't. Some go by the letter and are of course doomed to failure. Some go by the thrust of the thing and do not stick to the precision, the details, of the Plan, the exact moments and turns, and are of course doomed to failure. The Plan is composed with a sense of balance, a knowledge that there will be leeway, room for alternatives, improvisations, which intelligent executives will easily grasp, but which will elude those doomed to failure. But the Plan is composed with precision as stated. It must be precise inside of lassitude. It must be free, improvisational even, inside of precision. I reassert the Plan was perfect. Why things went as they did, I leave to your judgment.

THE MURDER OF GARCIA LORCA

> *No es sueño la vida.*
> *¡Alerta! ¡Alerta! ¡Alerta!*

I tug the strings of my fear, my bad puppet, Diablo, and tap him about this space, my first and last stage, last props, last lights, behind and in front of my painted screen. See, I pull up a leg and he hops, hops, hops! Who are you, Diablo? Herr Hitler, con permiso. Then hop, Hitler, hop! Garcia will be dead when I do this jig under the Arc de Triomphe. Not amusing, Diablo. Be something else. I want light and color! Then look at my gypsy dress, all layered, laced, ribboned, and brocaded—scarlet, gold, and green. Feel the wide wind of my rich fan. Hear my diamonded castanets! When did you put that on? An instant ago, behind the screen, when you were talking. But now I'll be Franco and rise against the Republic. Another ugly joke! But in an instant, true! Just let me don this uniform. I love good fun, but this is wicked. Night must fall, Federico, even if it frightens you. Diablo, I command you, take off that uniform, with its golden shoulder-mops and scrambled eggs and salads. I wish I could drop the reins of your dark horse. Who am I now? Wait, I recognize you. You're a man from my hometown, a *granadino*. Your name is . . . *Diablo!* Yes, and I am jealous of your genius. I call you out! I name you Red! *Red, red, red!* I am a poet. I hate politics. Nevertheless, I charge you, Federico Garcia Lorca, with crimes against the state . . . of my ego. And what now? Bang, bang, you're dead! Am I dead, Diablo? In an unmarked grave! Is it dark, Federico? No darker than this dark century, Diablo.

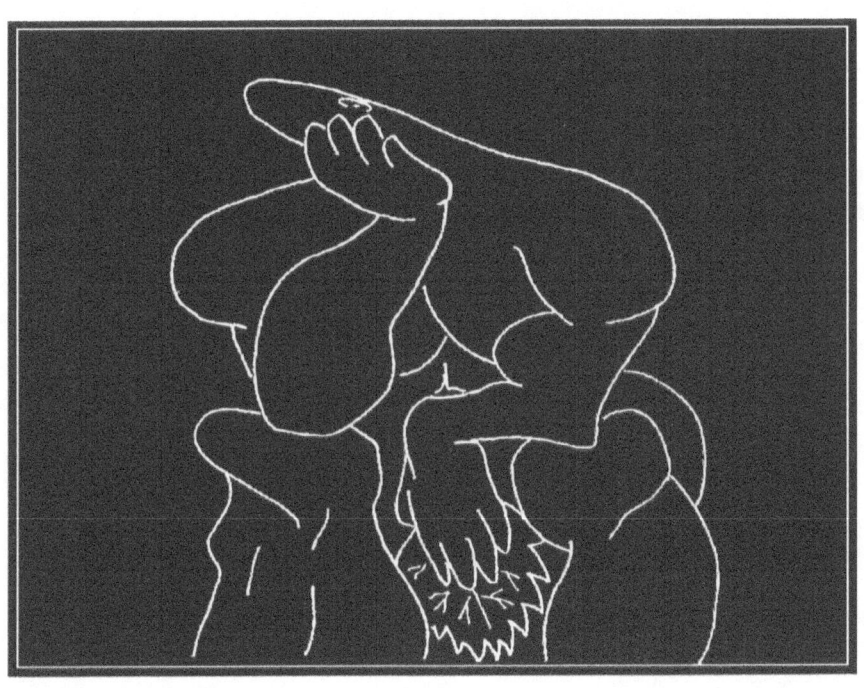

HUMANS, PEACE, AND THE RUMOR OF WAR

There is no war! Not over here, not over there, nowhere, in fact. There is no war and now we must ask ourselves the following questions: Whence come our new inventions? How are we to learn to pack food? Will the population explode? Will the over-taxed planet wither? And just as the questions were becoming hysterical cries, the old boom began again, on the far side of the quiet mountain, and the relieved people began to stand tall and sing their great songs of defiance, as if there had never been a moment of peace.

THE MARTYR

The heart of the true God would break for such fools. Christ would cry for them in their stupidity—husbands and wives signing away their homes; the old, the hard-handed scrawny, betraying their children for such as these plastic saints, with their radio and television towers rising all over the world, towers of their power, and time-shares for these poor-fool souls, to visit a plastic heaven and be regarded as its angels, like the angels of a Broadway Show, to shine in their pride before that great production—God's Follies. The impresario smiling out at them from his great stage knows they will not turn against him, for to do so would make heaven fall, would make him the devil of their days and them the devil's dupes. So, when he's exposed, when he has his Dies Irae, they march against the courts declaiming his innocence, proclaiming his martyrdom, while he hides under a bed and cries, and must be dragged out, and off to prison, the final soul-less product of materialism, eventually to return to the public stage, bringing a best-seller of his efforts at reform in a white-collar prison and, perversely, of his innocence and terrible martyrdom.

THE DOG SHOW

I have to take my master or mistress—or my "best friend"—and run one of them in a circle in front of the judges. Usually, it's my mistress whom I must run, and she has terrible coordination, often becoming entangled in the leash I pull her along with and tripping in front of the judges and the onlookers, causing me considerable embarrassment. I believe the person whom we lead is judged by what their clothing and jewels look like, and also possibly on their agility. It cannot be that they are judged by their physical assets, as most of the competitors are poor physical specimens indeed, with humps and lumps and bumps and other deformities aplenty. Also, most of them can't see very well, and none of them can detect the powerful odors backstage. Besides, we run too fast for them—especially if they wear lifted heels, as do many of the men. In their stage fright and general confusion at being onstage, they often drag their toupees along the floor, leaving us sitting on our haunches and laughing. Yes, dogs can laugh, too, and, as you can see, they can write as well.

DEATH ROW

In the Prison of the North, in some Bismarck of winter, the bars are ice, the walls are iceberg tips, and the guards steer past the cells on sleds of frozen water. Whiteness at night, with shadows behind each corner: thin cotton blankets to teach us a lesson, another lesson, one more than all the others. But Death Row is not a place, anymore than Purgatory, it's a waiting period, and we stand naked in it until, frozen, we fall, we fall and break, we shatter, we grit the floor like rice. Fire here is the touch of ice—we light our mentholated cigarettes with a touch of ice, with our own fingertips, our lost and blackened and found-again toes. We light our smokes with our frost-bitten, blackened toes and watch white paper burning back, turning black, and a red spark with its dark smoke vanish in the winter light. This is what we get for being what we are—monsters with icewater in our veins, cold-blooded killers of love, runaways. Neither does the prison of the North contain us, we contain it, got it young, most of us, got it and walk about with it freezing up inside us, got it and can't find warmth, don't remember how, and the worst of it is that we cannot even touch one another or we shatter. Do you hear that creaking sound? One of us has tried to touch another, the oh-so-lonely one we call The Refrigerator, has tried to find a friend, the friend he tried to find we call The Freezer. The Refrigerator sought love so savagely that he was iced in love's bipolar cell, and now his durance on Death Row is done.

CONFESSIONS

There was a young priest who stalked the pornographic night of the X-rated movie houses and the prostituting streets outside them in what had become a sexual compulsion. Sometimes he felt that he had lost all control of himself and with that loss his very soul. But his soul was saved through the confession of his sins and their forgiveness by a fellow priest who was not his own publicly acknowledged confessor but a fellow sinner, an older priest who had had a twenty-year quasi-marriage and who would in turn ask the young priest for absolution after confessing to him. When the young priest made confession to his acknowledged confessor and spiritual guide a little later, he had only to confess to the evil thoughts of the days since he last stalked the streets, thereby keeping his spiritual guide in the dark. He behaves as if in a dream when he is in the grip of this compulsion, as if he himself has become a character in the dirty movie he is watching, and in this state of disassociation picks up the first prostitute he sees, and, with release, becomes guilt-ridden and disgraced until he must seek out his secret-confessor. He will find a telephone within minutes of the event, plug in the number, wait, and say in a voice thick with mixed emotions of shame and anger, "I must see you." His secret confessor never refuses, no priest does, but he will take the confession with a heavy heart, for his friend and for himself. The confession, it seems, has become part of the compulsion, as both have come to suspect. Advice is traded, elements of which might have proven helpful to either priest, but none has been acted on, until . . .

CARPOOLING IT IN THE CARAVAN

Such amazement at reality as to make it seem unreal, and the knowledge of the confluence of disparate events, where impulsiveness and inventiveness meet, such amazement and such knowledge have sometimes thrilled me out of thought so that I must seem a victim of logorrhea in the library of life, gleaning a joke out of the quiet morning business commute, the one the serious morning newspaper readers want ejected from the carpool. Facts become treasures in an uncertain world. They are cheese to mice on a flying mudball. Since the past is deepest dark, and no binding statement concerning the future is possible, my fellow travellers engross themselves with the headlines and sports pages, ignorant of ultimate purpose, and, unlike me, content with now.

WILDER THAN WILDER

The Town Crier came by crying, "Time to get up and trash the day." Nonsense, the Town Crier is not an alarm clock, but the Town Crier *is* an alarm clock of sorts, so the townspeople rose and immediately prepared for the monkey war of all against all. While they were having coffee, they scowled at one another. A sister threw porridge at her little brother, the little brother pulled the cat's tail, and the cat scratched the dog. It was a typical morning. The Town Crier went home to his wife. "I have done my duty," he told her. "I have started the whole thing again." "One day," said his wife, "I am going to refuse to wind you up." They scowled at each other. The Mayor came to see the Town Crier. "I'm going to fire you," he said. "If it weren't for you waking the town every morning we shouldn't have all this strife." "I have a contract," said the Town Crier. "You have no authority to give me the chuck." Then the Doctor visited the Mayor. "What we must do," said the Doctor, "is to make the town sleep through the Town Crier's cry. I shall put a powerful drug in the water." "And the town will sleep peacefully all day long," cried the Mayor, seeing the merit of the Doctor's plan. So they tried it, and the town slept right through the Town Crier's cry. All but the Mayor and the Doctor and the Town Crier himself, who never drank water. The Town Crier came to complain to the Mayor because he couldn't wake anyone up and felt that he might lose his job. On the grounds that he was being neurotic, the Mayor sent him to the Doctor. The Town Crier stated his case, and, to his surprise, the Doctor agreed with him. "The fact is," said the Doctor,

"I have no patients—no broken bones to heal, no blackened eyes, no split lips, nothing to do all day. And the City Contractor is upset. He has nothing to repair. Let's go and have it out with the Mayor." So the Town Crier, the Doctor, the Fire Chief, and the City Contractor went to see the Mayor. The Mayor refused to see them, so they trashed his office, and, finding him hiding behind a file cabinet, they dragged him out into the town square and threatened to hang him. By this time everyone in town was wide awake. Quickly, a mob formed, ready to hang the Mayor. A riot ensued, and the town was torn apart. The City Contractor was very pleased. And when the mob set fire to the town, the Fire Chief was pleased to be busy again. "You tear it down, and I'll rebuild it," said the City Contractor to the Fire Chief. The Doctor said, "There will be injuries galore." A wife said something hateful to her husband, a sister to a brother, and a cat scratched a dog. The Town Crier cried, "Hear Ye, Hear Ye!" and life went on much as before.

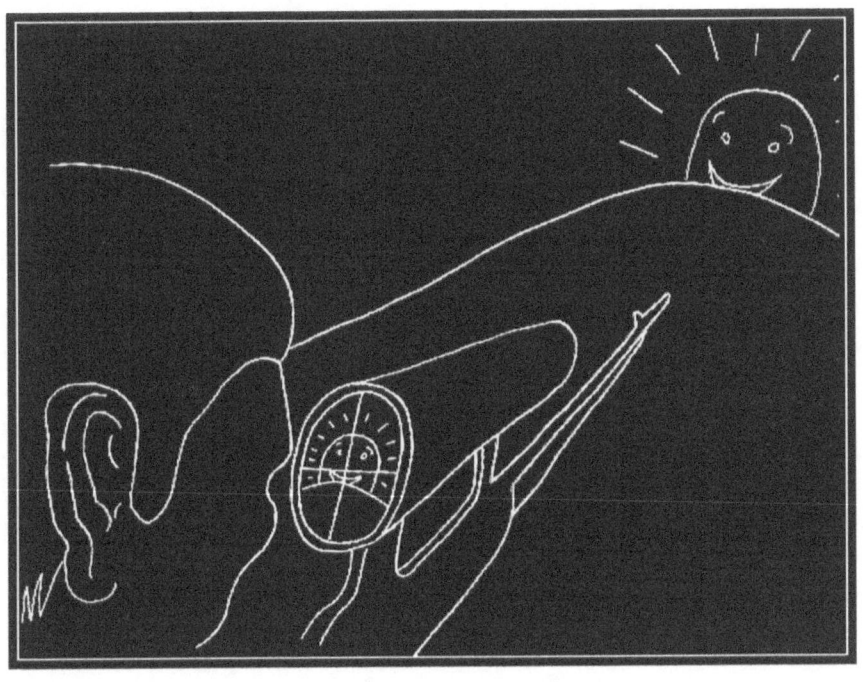

THE WAKE

The problem of the priest soliciting funds for the I.R.A. disturbs the likes of me who am only Irish on my mother's side. What would my grandfather, Joe McGrath, who went to England and later came on to the States and helped to make three children and died at the age of twenty-nine, say? Nothing, I guess, from the Pearly Gates; but since his nickname was "English," he might not have approved. The Irish whiskey is very tasty, though, and the boiled food isn't bad, especially the spuds. The Brooklyn priest is packing a rod. I can see it clear as the smiling moon, poking out his dark garb up high at the shoulder. Does he think the rest of us are blind to a pistol grip? He'd say it was to protect the Collect, now that he's older and can't go bare hand like he done as a Borstal boy. So it's money for the bombs and the poor dead soul lying over there ignored! But he was a member himself, though he never did more than to knock at the door, like one of them that is always coming by and asking for a handout. And that's just what the gun-toting priest is saying now—that it's a good cause, and you can guess which cause it is—and I wonder if he's a priest at all or if he's just been released from some asylum in upstate New York. Ah, here's the dead's good wife, now. Hard as nails she is but still she does her proper share of the keening, disposing of the task with what you could call, "sure and begorrah," an iron will.

THE URN

It is this heavenly tale, that the child in one could wish for, that keeps me awake tonight, on the eve of my sixtieth year, fearing death and wishing for grace, not knowing what either is, or even if either is, though the unbreathing stillness of bodies has me fairly convinced of the former, and of the latter I have seen so little as to doubt what I have seen as aberrant, some twist in the air and light that, so full of desire for the magic of exemption, I have deluded myself, half knowing I lied, half believing my own white lie. But by sixty I've come to believe that the only grace is the goodness of the rational mind, and the only evil the old instinctive animal brain, the knob of the cerebellum, seeking its own satisfactions of food and sex and selfhood, the ultimate isolate one, that yet does not understand that we are together in this flowing, amazing hologram, with or without a creator that may or may not care; that, come alive, we have every right to judge the nature of existence, for, however arrived at, our brains are analytic, not made to hunker down in obeisance to riddling gods, nor to any phantom that hides in a cloud of unknowing. For we have one another and have courage and the hope of courage and the practice of courage, to help us, and, when the wind is calm, and the waters lean down for the moon, we have lonely senses to share till at last our time has run out. Now, as I think in the night, somewhat afraid of the day that will see me another year older and that much closer to death, I mark the speed of time that has seen me, a moment ago, a child walking home from school, or a man going off to harm's way, or this or that or the other, and think of these things that we have, of others and courage and love, of human intelligence used as it plainly was meant to be used, and I think that I'll sleep and awaken less anxious than I was considering a heavenly tale, for in the realist reality, the closest thing to the truth, there is finally a peace of mind that is a grace in a sweet surrender. It is the heavenly tale that the child in one should wish for. *It* will allow me to sleep in the night of my sixtieth year.

THE TERRIBLE SHADOW

Mind free of the terrible shadow of death, the child, who had gathered itself in the womb and could no longer remember its long genetic history, nor the gunmetal black un-time before it, sprang forth and grew until a time came when a whisper of futurity touched its quivering nerves; but still, mind free of the terrible shadow of death, felt by its mother and father, the child played in a place of organic magic, eating gummy worms and studying the dirt forming under its nails; now, mind free of the terrible shadow of death, the child attended the properly appointed and appropriate schools at each required stage, suffering often, but often joyful beyond adult reason—a bright kite flew, an airplane left a jet trail, a rainbow appeared out of the blue—and the shadow began to form, the terrible shadow of death. Mind no longer free of the terrible shadow of death, the child wrinkled like an overripe fruit, grew old, felt the terrible shadow of death, and died; then, no more mind, the child became the shadow.

ROUSSEAUVIANS

They found their ideal in the rain forest of the Amazon, these scientific photographers from National Geographic; they found a tribe of twelve scarred and bitten people who lived naked and ate monkeys which they shot out of trees with blowguns. They knew that they had finally found the Noble Savage. But romance backs away from finality, and they took their pictures and returned to their dry homes in Georgetown, deploring the modern urban life and declaiming for all to hear how they had found the perfect life and left it behind in order to bring it to the public.

POWERITUS

"It is pandemic and dates from the cavepeople," the doctor said. "Working in the Emergency Room, I see it every day. Alexander-the-Great-itus, Napoleonic fever, Hitlerian jaundice, Capone's inflammation of the vanity, call it what you will. I say it is pandemic only to indicate how broad a spectrum suffers from it. Actually, it is genetic. A recessive gene, it keeps popping out where you least expect it. *Poweritus!* That nervous little artistic boy over there may have his doodles rejected. He will appear later in league-boots, brandishing a sword, merciless. He will kill ten million people before he is stopped or dies of natural causes. That young actress in Argentina. Beware of those who have a vision for you. It is not natural to have a vision for other people. One should have one's own vision for oneself. It is a horrifying disease. If it is genetic, it is a recessive gene, and you or I, or anyone, might be the victim of it, and make us all victims of it in small or, heaven help us, large ways. Thank God it only afflicts humans. To my knowledge, there has never been an animal afflicted with Poweritus. What if a truly powerful species were infected with it?" "Why do they write biographies of these diseased creatures?" I asked. "Casebooks," said the doctor. "Casebooks, and the envy of a few effete historians!"

THE GENIUS FLIGHT

The Village became tired of supporting the Village Idiot, partly because he was demanding and partly because he was surly. The Village Leaders got together and came up with a scheme to rid themselves of the surly and demanding Village Idiot, to wit: they would send him to Congress. With the support of the Village, his Congressional District elected him. Now the Village Idiot was a Congressman. They gave him a party, after which they took him to the airport to catch his plane. Now it happens that the flights that take New Members of Congress to Washington are called Genius Flights, because half way to Washington from whatever point the New Congressperson becomes a genius. When they land at Washington, they know all there is to know about every subject imaginable, and so with the Village Idiot sent to Congress by his Village because he was demanding and surly, suddenly he became an Expert on Everything. He belongs to the Committee on Agriculture and the Committee on Finance and, most interesting of all, to the Committee on Intelligence, so who says Anyone can't make it in America?

MANNERS, MANNERS

Convention dictated that two people meeting in the street should knock their heads together in greeting, so Smirnoff banged his forehead into Zubov's, but, in his enthusiasm for formality, did not wait for Zubov to remove his hat and bang him back. Zubov therefore fell to ground in a semiconscious state, and Smirnoff had to help him to his feet. Manners, said Zubov, recrimination ringing in his voice, Manners. Smirnoff had Zubov standing now. A thousand pardons, he said. He held the swaying Zubov upright. Get my hat, please, said Zubov, pointing to the hat, which had rolled off into the gutter. Smirnoff let go of Zubov's shoulders and got the hat. He returned, spitting on the hat and brushing it with his sleeve, to find that Zubov had retreated to the ground and lay spreadeagled. This time Zubov had cracked the back of his head open and lay in a pool of blood. Just then another couple bumped heads, and both went down. Smirnoff shook his own large head, from the front of which a red welt was making an appearance. Our culture is too much bound by convention, he said in disgust, dropping the hat by Zubov's body, and going on about his business.

ME AND MY SHADOW

One day my shadow walked away. The air seemed filled with gold and silver microdots, a bright sandslide. I had to hold my hand over my eyes for the glare. But I could see my shadow, up ahead. It turned around and looked at me, and that was when I first noticed that it had turned from a dark shadow to a light one, silver-gray, in fact, and was growing even more pale. "You don't need me anymore," my shadow said. "But of course I need you," I said. "It wouldn't be the same without you." "But don't you see what is happening?" said my shadow. "Isn't your chest just a bit tight?" Traffic boomed by. And yes, I did feel a bit tight in the chest. "You see," said my shadow, "I want to get on with my own business." "What business have you got that excludes me?" I demanded to know. "Do you have indigestion? Are you breaking out in a sweat? Do things look a bit strange to you?" Why, yes, the gold and silver microdots were swarming, as in a sand storm, a simoon, and they had lost a great deal of their color, becoming glass-like, and they were causing my skin to itch. I summoned up what energy I had and ran several steps ahead, into my shadow, and tried to stay there. Then a man came by and said, "There is a dead man here," and walked briskly on. I found myself beside him, ahead of him, behind him. I have been shadowing him ever since—I can't help it—but I have found that he leads a very hard life, so I would have hope for the future but for the fact that I don't know where my own shadow went.

THE PRODUCER

I agree that you should make this movie, which we shall entitle Life. But if it is to be about life, it must have versimilitude. I should go about it like this: The Script. Should be written by an illiterate madman or madwoman. Maybe a team. The Director. Should be a hopeless drunk, or a drug addict. The Producer. The name one dare not speak. The stars. Simian, male and female. The rest of the cast. Insane, greedy, and stupid. The cop who watches over things. Crooked. The city. Any city, just as it is. The equipment. Faulty. The set. A place where there is a great deal of spent nuclear waste. Extra dialogue. The oink, oink sound. Conflict. That will take care of itself. Excuse me, it's time for my pills. Now I think you are ready to proceed.

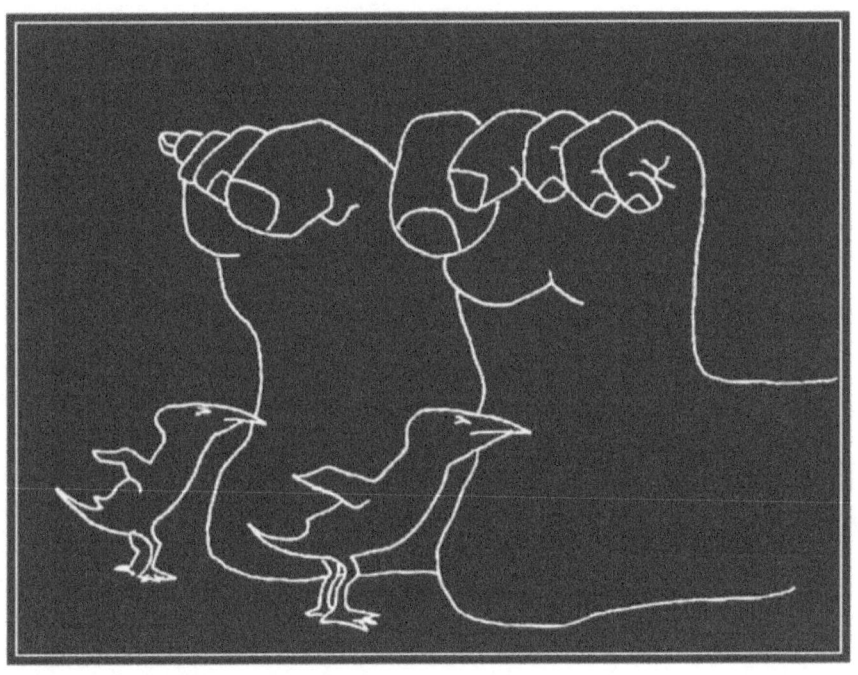

BAD TRIP

I noticed what beautiful teeth the young man had. Mine are missing or turned to coffee, red wine, and smoke. The hitchhiker had a seabag stencilled with my name. I have an unusual name and it could not have been sheer coincidence. I was going west—he said west was fine. The Mojave highway was empty for as far as I could see. I stopped the car. He tried to open the door, but I had them all locked. I shot him, then unlocked the doors and pushed his body out into the roadside sand. I got out and rolled him out of view, down a sand dune, and buried him, dust to dust. Well, I might as well have done so, even if I didn't. What I did to him was nearly as bad, maybe worse. I let him live and become me. So most of my life I have been living inside a much younger man. It was quite an adventure, being young. He ran a lot, ran long distances and very short, marathons and dashes. He got embarrassing erections on buses, hanging onto the strap, and would have to face away in a twisted posture, but the rest of him, being loose, not stiff, he could contort and hide his secret lust. In middle age, he was big-voiced and positive, sure of everything, in a way I find impossible; I, who doubt all. I have many photographs of him. Lifting barbells. Boxing. He is always glad to pose. Myself, I hate having my picture taken. It is certain to come back to me as an old fart, grinning stupidly at the camera, as if to say, "I am still like him, like that hitchhiker." But I am not just like him, not at all like him, inside or out. I miss him but don't want him back. I would rather crawl forward and under; for, now that I think about it, he never was so hot, never the number he thought he was.

DARK CANZONE

From when some wandering primate first discovered that vocal cords had formed within its throat: when thorax wind was blown, and it discovered a modulation of its grunts, discovered it had a tongue that could articulate more subtly than it had presumed; discovered, in fact, its ur-humanity; discovered that it was different from monkeys, wiser, and could communicate a plan; was wiser, one than the other, in this gift; discovered, in short, itself as special being, poet, it sang in lamentation for the poet, O felt itself the oddest ape, a poet, and, with the weight of what it knew, discovered the truest nature of itself as poet, that it must bear the burden of the poet, harsh bile of truth that rises in the throat and burns the vocal cords of every poet. For meaning murders innocence, the poet learns, word by word; and to articulate as in a grammar, to articulate as words demand, and so to be a poet is to be that most special being, stranger than any other animal—but wiser? It felt itself the strangest thing, much stranger than any other animal—a poet—for words had made it thuswise stranger. But was it better being this much wiser? What had this primate after all discovered? Who really thinks it's better to be wiser? Who doesn't know it's sadder to be wiser? Who envies words blown through a poet's throat? What poet hasn't wished to cut its throat? If grammar makes for meaning, is it wiser to be a special being, to articulate the truth words find—or not articulate? It may be braver to articulate, to be an animal, yet strangely wiser, but is it wisdom to articulate the grunts of animals, articulate from them the existential life of poet among the primates, to articulate—

syntactically commanded—articulate the place in nature that we have discovered, the death in nature that we have discovered? Grunt one last grunt! Enough! Articulate no more! Oh, envy nothing from the throat of any poet! Let it cut its throat! Oh, let the primate poet cut its throat before it's forced on to articulate, by sending lamentations through its throat, from its self-fabled heart and out its throat, how truly sad it is to be a little wiser than other animals that have a throat but have no vocal cords within that throat which they can use to make themselves a poet who sings the lamentations of a poet, a sadder wiser primate prophet poet, whose ordered language has at last discovered what happy animals have not discovered . . . . What is it animals have not discovered, which leaves them happier than any poet? The ordered thought of death! It might be wiser for nature never to articulate; wisest, to stay mere stone.

SAFETY

Auto seatbelts started it, the quest for safety. Now on a golden sunny day on a walk in town, up and down the sidewalks we go, strapped to pulley belts to help us get from store to store. Now we have belts on our bicycle seats and, when we crash, we crash with the bike tangled to us. We have belts on our toilets, our commodes, our W.C. seats, so that we can't get off in time to beat the overflow. We are strapped to our desks, we who work at desks, and strapped to our beds at night, unable to make love. Our children walk on ever-shorter leashes. Our dogs are tied to trees. Only our cats have escaped this safety and continue to live dangerously. Airbags are compressed into our steering wheels. But I don't understand how they get a politician into a steering wheel, or how he or she stays alive in there, not that I care.

DETOUR
for Sue

Up and down, the far hills come to me as if summoned by a time machine from the speed-unlimited future, and, on lonely stretches, by night, I hit the high beams and drive in a domed glow, hoping to be taken for a flying saucer travelling low in the long dark of the cartoon map's flyover country, wild hares leaping. Eventually, I stop for food at the Roadkill Diner that I find at least once in every state. I stoke up and drive on, warm in the cold weather of a constant late autumn, my body comfortable, forgettable, so that my mind can sit atop the car like a beacon, a blue light with a soft, humming siren, the streamline of wind, while my hands steer the roadshapes, and see, occasionally, along the road a dead possum, rabbit, skunk or squirrel, and, once, lately, the much-impacted carcass of a deer, the road spatter-painted a raging red, and look back to be sure of what I have seen, and then ahead again, which in my case, on this particular trip, diverted, detoured by cell-phone, is to the burial of a friend, as I enter her state with brakes down for a speedtrap, and a black and white patched and ribboned sky overhead.

THE TRUE MEANING OF *ARMIDE*

The overt message of Gluck's tragedy is that it is more dangerous to love than to be loved, but that simplicity is not the true meaning of *Armide*. Rinaldo had a strong arm and a brave heart, but Armide had all the power of magic at her disposal. How could she have failed to win her way? She failed because, in loving Rinaldo, it became impossible for her to use her power against him, love rendering the powerful helpless before the object, no matter how weakened that object. If Rinaldo had loved Armide as she loved him, there should have been no tragedy, but a tale of domestic bliss, one utterly unsuitable for the public's appetite for mayhem and murder, or, in this case, for fiery suicide. More than enough about humanity is told when it is said that *Armide* remains Gluck's masterpiece, nearly as popular today as when it was first produced in Paris at the Académie Royal de Musique, in 1777, for a bloodthirsty culture that couldn't wait for heads to roll.

RX: THE FLOWER CURE

Cerato for self-doubt, a cause of sexual dysfunction. Mix with Aspen. Make a tea. Gentian leaves relieve depression. Make a broth with a dash of Sweet Chestnut. Also, for gloom and melancholia, Mustard Flowers. Impatiens for impatience. Make a soup of gold, add black olives to allay mental fatigue, and Hornbeam for decrepitude. Then go to the Hollybush for vigor. If your love remains indifferent, offer a few sips of Clematis. But heed this, lover, heed this: Take your love into the country and pick these flowers together!

WINNERS

Skulls seem to take pride in their bald hollowness, like grinning Halloween pumpkins. Have you ever seen one roll down from the top of a pile, like those piles that Pol Pot used to stack? Vanity-free, it is no less content at the bottom than it was at the top. It may rest there, upside down, and frown; but, right side up, it would still be wearing the same silly smile: all that is needed for you to see that smile is for you to stand on your head, or, to set it upright. And all skulls look pretty much alike. Some are a little elongated, some are flat on top, or bullet-shaped, but they are all pretty much the same, when unsupported by spines, and fallen to the lowest point of gravity's pull. Always they smile inanely, like poor country folk who have won the lottery. "Cheer up," they seem to say, "the best is yet to come."

A FABLE

It seems there is a place where beggars and poor people go to tell tales, and the mostly riding moon will park to look and to listen in the dark to the tales as they are told by the poor beggar bards of the hobo jungle, a place lonely as life, at the end of the track, in a cul-de-sac of starred, campfired night, in a turntabled copse in the dark ragged green of smoke-stunted oak and rope-strong weeds, where birds bivouac: and of all beggar bards who sang a sad ballad there, for the folk, or chanted a moon-watched tale, the most famous because most magical was the hobo bard the Pinkertons called "The All-Seeing Eye," because of his blind, superhuman vigilance, and the mooncalf folk called "O'Shay the Irish Shaman" for his gift of curative power, uncanny control of events, and for divining the deep, hooded meaning of things beyond their poor eyes and plain powers to see.

Now O'Shay rose up and loomed before them, above them, his flame-mapped face red and changing as the cat-o'-nine-tailed fire, his great, blind eyes like those of the horse of his inner-eye (a carp-eyed stallion), his hair a red, swimming flame dowsed by the cool waters of the moon. O'Shay, though blind, was free, though poor, was proud, and did not like to see the poor folk bowed by that boulder, Care, nor bullied by the railroad dicks and afraid in their camp at the end of the track underneath the parked moon in the starred, turntabled copse where he loomed now, watching their weak eyes with his strong, inner one, and knowing that they needed a hopeful tale to be told that the Depression be lifted, courage restored, and the parked moon set free to ride the night into dawn, and new hope for them, crying: "Pride's the subject of my moon-watched tale. Now listen to O'Shay, poor people, and see what you think—stop, look, and listen with the fascinated moon.

"There was a white stallion that lived when you were still babes of scuttlebutt at heaven's height, and that full, silver moon itself unborn of the great, swaying sea; a stallion of clouds and spirit that came finally to gallop the great plains of the North American west; a pale, proud, bellows-nostrilled, carp-eyed king of a horse, that could blow back the floozy wind from Manitoba down to the plains of old Mexico; that could whinny across the west to call a brood mare from her happy home to him a thousand miles away in the night; that spoke in trumpeting tongues of his freedom, stamped, and neighed pride from his great, rampant heart; who hammered hope with his hooves to the ranging mustangs of the plain. A maverick king, he! And this is the best part, for the horse was blind like myself, and nothing daunted, unconstrained, for he saw with his four, steamed, cow-catcher hooves, and his ears that could hear the baby-breath sigh of a willow on an unborn wind; saw, too, and best, with an inner eye like my own, and had powers, like myself, gifts of nature, with which he could divine the treachery of humankind, and thus keep himself free, and wear no man's hot brand.

"For he wore no man's brand; and that was a heartache to all rich ranchers who had heard of the white stallion: his freedom mocked their staked, barbed wire; and they offered gold for his capture—pots of rainbow gold those rich ranchers offered the buck who captured the stallion; gold, gold beyond a poor cowpoke's wildest dreams, fifty thousand dollars in gold bullion to the buckaroo who brought in the phantom of the prairies, fifty more to the bronco buster who broke him—fifty thousand in gold, one hundred thousand in gold bars to do both! They came from the stretched limbs of the continent—wranglers, roustabouts, beggars and poor people like ourselves, all with mad schemes to capture the blind, white stallion, keen on the trace of gold." Here O'Shay's brick jaws mortised, his lips ringed teeth, and his dark sockets fixed face after face, saw! And yet they knew O'Shay was a blind man and could not see the mad excitement they felt, hearing of gold, could not see how they stood who had sprawled or hunkered down on their heels here, could not know, therefore, how ready for pursuit they were, how each in his mind saw a fleece-white phantom flee his grasp, as O'Shay took pause from his moon-watched tale, and they cried out to him, as one many-voiced, to go on.

"Mad men with mad schemes!" cried O'Shay. "For they knew, the earthly fame of the phantom being, by now, widespread, that all the ordinary methods of capture had been tried and had failed. No, a ghost must be caught in some other way. Hence these mad or tragic traps. One loon dreamed of speeding hoopsnakes that would ensnarl the steed's cow-catcher hooves, another's gold-frenzy fancied a fast balloon. The supernatural horse and the idea of gold had made them mad. Not all, some had sounder brains and better schemes. A wrangler, a strong man who knew his horses, had staked out an arroyo which was a haunt of the white steed. He pitched camp and waited; and happenstance his patience was rewarded when, like a mirage, the pale, maverick king, with his own remuda of mares prancing and curvetting behind, galloped up to drink, stamping and snorting. The wrangler climbed a rise, and, twirling an Indian-charmed lariat of rawhide interwoven with shot-gold wire, which he had bought from a Kiowa shaman, roped him, looping the golden noose neatly around his neck. The white stallion whinnied, rose rampant, and snapped the charmed, magic lasso as the wrangler might have snapped a golden thread; and the still-noosed stallion and his mares vanished in white dust. But this was the closest that any man had come. News of his failure spread up and down the plains, told by range riders on lonely duty tours, at starred, campfired night, until word reached a famed trapper up in Manitoba, one who had trapped every kind of animal. His name was Hawkeye Red.

"Hawkeye Red," he said, "left his cold northern home and journeyed far southwest to find the white stallion. Then he methodically began work on his great trap. He gathered the strongest oaken lumber that could be found and built a great stable in the arroyo where the horse was golden-noosed, and in it placed the most beautiful young mare that the rich ranchers possessed among them, a doe-eyed, blazed-faced bay with black mane and tail. Ringbolt-tethered, high-strung, frightened, Bonny-Pru would be the bait. Now he set the trap doors, cleverly contrived to clap shut behind the white stallion when, or if, he entered, trapping him. Hawkeye

Red and the rich ranchers retired to a vantage point to wait for the phantom of the plains.

"Under the riding moon, Bonny-Pru pulled, kicked the oaken planks, and whinnied for her freedom across the dappled night, until her fearful, fearsome cries were borne as on an unborn wind to the white steed. The man-watched moon rode high as the hours passed and nearer and nearer he galloped with all his magical might toward her in her trap, and his; but at last he came to the dark and looming stable; and, though the great, mouthing doors gaped open, paused, galloped away, circling wide the foreboding building; then, though he knew this was a trap, galloped in to the distressed, stable-trapped, ringbolt-tethered damsel mare who cried out for a brave champion like himself. The trap doors shut! Silence! No sound whatever from inside the stable. The rich ranchers whooped high for their victory; but, somehow, Hawkeye Red, now rich, felt saddened by his success. All left their vantage point and approached the stable. But, nearing it, the doors split, splintered like kicked glass, spilled, filled the spiked air, and up and over the heads of Hawkeye Red and the rich ranchers rose the white steed and his damsel mare like two wide-winged, magical, legendary birds. Hawkeye Red shook his head in unbelief, turned, dazed, to see them, bullets that followed the riflings of infinity. In a moment of wild, unholy desperation, he ran to his horse, reached for his rifle, aimed, and fired.

"The rifle exploded, but from the breech, not the muzzle, blinding him. And in that first blind instant he saw the horse of his mad pride go free, the white phantom rise rampant and neigh, like a musical muscle that flexes and sings, and vanish from the land, with his blazed-faced bride, Bonny-Pru, by his side, never to return." The poor people were on their feet, now, whinnying, and galloping in place, for O'Shay had turned them into happy horses who would wear no man's brand, who applauded their pleasure with hoof-clap hands and tongues that rode the roofs of moon-watched mouths. "Hawkeye Red," he said, "regained his vision, but saw no more with his outer eyes, but with a strong, inner one, and lived to tell the tale at the end of a track, in a cul-de-sac of starred, campfired night, in a turntabled copse in the dark, ragged green of smoke-stunted oak and rope-strong weeds, where birds bivouac."

And he set the moon free.

THE ASSASSIN AND THE SCARAB

The assassin waited in a high window, his bulging left green eye like an egg in an eggcup, drowned by an eyecup, which was the near end of his telescopic sight, below which protruded and projected a laser's arrowlight blue nose that scanned the facade of a gray public building, its blue dot finale hovering here and there, then jumping two or three feet, this way and that. The assassin had been waiting too long for his quarry to emerge and was growing tired and impatient. Some kind of beetle kept batting at him. He batted back, and the beetle fell to the window sill, just beyond his tripod. He sucked his eye out of his telescope and looked at the beetle, which lay on its back, flapping its wings. Its stomach was iridescent silver and gold, a beautiful nugget. "Here," said the assassin, turning the beetle over, "let me see the rest of you. Why, you're gorgeous! Yes, all gold, and what a gold you are! Old gold—something from the Renaissance. Or you could have been the original Egyptian scarab." The assassin jumped back as the beetle leaped into the air, flapping its golden wings. It landed where the blue light emerged from the laser beam on the assassin's highly tooled and polished weapon. Then the assassin saw his quarry emerge from the building across the way. Into the sight went his green left eye, like an egg in an eggcup, or indeed an eye drowned in an eyecup, and there was the blue dot, about a hundred yards away, like a bug on the wall of the gray public building. He shifted the dot toward his quarry's heart, and at that instant saw something odd: a bit of gold travelling down the blue beam like a child on a sliding board. The beetle landed on the heart of the assassin's quarry. The quarry stepped aside, brushing the beetle from his chest. The bullet followed the blue line to the gray wall—smacked into it. The beetle picked up the blue beam and followed it back up to the assassin. The assassin grabbed the glittering beetle from the tip of the laser sight and put it in his pocket, then made his escape.

DATES AND DREAMS

A friend of mine had a datebook bulging with countless appointments not one of which was for pleasure. Medical-dental led the list (I am his doctor), then there were hundreds for business meetings. Holidays seemed to tumble from a cornucopia of guilt which only gifts could mitigate. All these appointments, he said, were blue raindrops, which he ran between, which he had been running between for as long as he could remember. Names, numbers, dates, times, seemed a plague of distractions to this man, who, it seemed, could never get to the point of his own life, which existed in its ultimate form in a second datebook, which was not a datebook at all, but was, or was meant to be, in practice, the repository of his more poetic thoughts, and which remained a book mainly filled with blank pages. My friend finally held the two books, one in each hand, as if weighing them against each other, and asked me which book he should throw away. Of course I have no way of knowing what he finally decided to do, but he missed our last appointment, and none of our common acquaintances has seen him in quite some time. I was treating him for high blood pressure. Now that he no longer comes to see me, he probably has time to write in his previously blank, poetic notebook, and I expect that his blood pressure has gone down with every entry.

WEBSITES

Life.org

A virus has more organized life than a star, though a star has an order of appearance, star in the sky and star on stage, but I am speaking of organic life, though a star on the stage or a movie star has organic life, more, in fact, than the virus. This explanation is paradoxical, a seeming contradiction, but let it stand for something in the same way that anything can stand for something else, particularly among symbolists and surrealists. In the same sense that the paranormal is most normal, the surrealists are most real. But humans are coelenterates: my liver heaves, my bowels twist, squirm with excitement and lead their own lives inside me. I need a new part. It pulsates. It is not my friend, but perhaps we can get along, after a time. At first, other parts reject it, but eventually they are tamed. You are all working for me, I cry. We are our own liver, kidney, heart. I am not your heart. You have no heart. Your better half told you that. You have no other half. It is all a golden fiction, inspired by sex. Your sex organs aren't even your own—they do as they please. As the real estate agent told the homeowner who questioned him about an easement, you don't own property, you control it. You don't own yourself, and you barely control yourself for social reasons of benefit to you and to the group. Life is the opposite of what is burning out there in space, that celestial snow, those flickering fireflies, which, close up, are all titanic violence. Life is soft and squirms when you caress it, and it could rule the night of the stars, if given time.

Death.com

I think of Earth as a great piñata, stuffed with death. Traditionally, at the end of the party, you take a whack at a piñata and it breaks, spilling its contents. If you did that with Earth, the countless dead would be released and scattered into space, and, though the geologists and the astrophysicists would disagree with me, I say that what would be left would be a tenth the size of the present globe, a wrinkled, raisin-like, bag that no longer had an orbit or an axis on which to fall toward the sun or to do its wobbly spin. The dead from Earth's beginnings to the present, or what was left of them, would float off into space, much as the stars, the galaxies are floating off, away from each other, red-shifted, and growing lonelier and lonelier. But perhaps there is something to meet somewhere out there. Perhaps the universe has a bright side. The darkness of the void wouldn't bother the remanents of the dead, they are used to it. They are as blind as they were when they lived, for we see with our minds not our eyes. So the whole thing is for the living. Death. Commercial. Stand in the midst of life and look at them go, to bones, to smoke, to ashes; then rejoin the matter of the universe yourself; the universe that, if it were capable of hope, could only hope to live.

THE FIDDLER

Played the devil's fiddle, stomping to it, shaking it out, full of corned blood, his boot down down down! Days before the corn, his old bitch Lucy lay by his piston heel. Said later she smelled it, stayed by it, waiting for the meaty bone; said later never done him no harm at all; said later not even a ghost of evil but Lucy got it, old bloodhound bitch like red clay, wrinkled old lady hanging from her own bones—could make her moonhowl, pointing his wild bow—do that at dances. Devil in a Baptist, playing the fiddle. Gradual as the mountains, he found out how the devil got in. Fiddle under his spiked, gray chin, corn jug thumb-hooked and cradled on top his elbow—capful for Lucy—then stomp stomp stomp: music through Blue Ridge pines! Could choo choo it so's you see smoke and steam, hear that wheezy accordion whistle; could conjure with it up a trainload of places or turn you back home to the station of pines and blue smoke mountains, bring musical rain, or put the devil in your heart, winking and drinking and stomping. Everybody loved him and his Lucy, including said devil, as the corn dropped down into his right big toe. Said it hurt to stomp. But it don't stop the fiddler. Don't nothing stop the fiddler! He was one thing else than music; he was a man. Take more'n corn going through, dropping down in my right big toe, says at the May dance, everybody seeing him stomp, ouch ouch ouch on his big red gray spiked old corned face. Devil got in through the corn, slick as silk; got down in my boot, but I'll stomp him out; give old Satan a headache—stomp stomp stomp! But that corn went to killing him. His bow was flying! Went on like this, folks say, a tad's five year, him stomping the devil in the corn and the devil stomping back. Said now he couldn't play no more if he don't get rid o' that old devil. Takes him a broad wood chisel out back on a stump, sets his right foot up, sets that chisel to his toe, and strikes down with a good hefty hammer. When he pulls back his foot, that devil in the corned toe stays on the stump, says looka me, I'm off! Has brought him some fireplace soot and some gingham. Sticks that foot in that black soot, to staunch the blood, and wraps it in gingham rags. Said never done him no harm again, quiet as a bone, and he goes back to stomping in peace, rid of the devil. But first, he throws that old corned toe to Lucy. Says: I knowed you always wanted it. Now mind the nail, Lucy; don't let the devil get you, you drunk old droop-skinned hound bitch, cuz I love you. And Lucy goes to lickin' that toe, pops it in, and goes to grinding up that devil in her old ground down chops. And next time we see them, the fiddler and his drunk bitch, they both full of corn, and ready, now, for the dance!

THE MAKEOVER

Sheets in pink and blue and wearing shadows and polkadots of red surrounded him. Come down from the ceiling! called the Board Certified plastic surgeons. Come back from the tunnel! cried the nurses. They were ironing his chest. If he had not been shaved, he'd have smelled the scorching hair. Zap! And he gave them that shiteaten expression he always wore when he was in trouble. I've got a pulse! cried a nurse. And then he remembered his fabulous visit to the other side. It was "a clean, well-lighted place," and the nurses were there, naked. No doctors allowed. The nurses sat at his feet, begging his attention. He's our fat Buddha, one said. Oh, my, but his now thirty-inch waistline hurt! They must have sucked fifty pounds of fat out of him. He saw a tube full of thick yellow syrup, a tube full of cheeseburgers, actually, and chocolate bars, and French fries, probably. His blood pressure is stabilizing! Look at that waistline, said a nurse. And the jowls are flat, now. Shall we start tucking that skin? Look at that butt! Good enough to eat! He's going to be beautiful! Too bad his heart had to stop. This is not an exact science, said a doctor. It's an art. Speaking of art, said the chubby nurse, I liked him when he was a character actor on that soap opera "The Sadder Day." I like him now, said a nurse who looked like a model. He was gone for over five minutes, said a doctor. We'll probably be sued. Brain damage, you know. I don't care if he *is* stupid, said the nurse who looked like a model, I'm taking him home with me. Everybody laughed. His wife, mother, and five daughters are waiting to hear how he is. Well, tell them he's lost fifty pounds and a lot of I.Q. and will probably get a divorce as soon as he can find his way to a lawyer, said the head doctor. That's what I would do, if I had his looks and no brains left. And a beautiful new profile. And an enlarged penis. And a flat gut. And a tight ass. And a plastic chin. I told you, said the nurse who looked like a model, I'm taking him home with me—dumb schmuck, but what a handsome hunk!

A SECOND CHILDHOOD

It was her birthday, but how could such a child read her birthday card, how could she enjoy her birthday cake? She was too young to read and wanted suckle, wanted to be held in arms and warm breast and find the nipple of life and the warm milk. The card was blurry and the cake was too rich. The nurses should quickly wrap her in warm blankets, lest she get a chill. But everyone must look at her, must look and say Good. "How bald she is," one said. "How tiny," said another. "Look, her eyes are stuck shut," said a third. She could not bear the pain of their attention, birthday or not. She began to cry. There was just a sigh with which to accompany her tears, but now her voice burst on their ears with a long, high-pitched cry. "We must take her away now and wash her and put her to beddy-bye," said the head nurse. And the relatives left the nursing home in several cars, another birthday under their belts, wondering if there should be yet another in the year to come.

THE REMAINDER MAN

There is a certain kind of Last Will and Testament where property is passed back to those who had claim to it before, but should they die, then it is passed on to a next of kin, even where the consanguinity extends to those who are completely unknown to the original possessor of the riches. It is something like a tontine, but not quite the same. The remainder man or woman is off somewhere and a true stranger to those at the center of things. Now there is a murder. And now another. The detective in charge knows what is happening, of course. He checks the records. He is trying to see who is next in line. But before he can find out, that person is murdered. Who is next, then? And how far does this family extend? After five hundred murders, the detective is exhausted. He applies for a leave of absence, which is fine as far as his superiors are concerned. They have been getting a very bad press, as you can imagine. Five hundred and one. Who is next? Who is the remainder man? Or woman? He or she may be on the other side of the world. Interpol is doing its best. The problem is that this is the world's most extended family. Cousins by the score. Then an aunt turns up in Denmark. Then an uncle in Cuba. It's maddening. Six hundred and seven and still counting. There is a huge sum of money involved. Billions. But this must be the most murderous family in history. A computer analysis finds that there are still over a million relatives. It turns out that the detective is related to the family. So are his superiors. The Queen of England is a relative. Scotland Yard has its suspicions. The F.B.I. is looking into the President's family tree. Could the Queen be the last, surviving remainder woman, or the President of the United States the last surviving remainder man? The Queen dies under suspicious circumstances. A-ha! Then the President falls off a balcony. Mmm! The Secretary of the Treasury was standing directly behind him. But he drops dead of shock. There is only one potential remainder person left, an unborn child whose mother, who is not in the blood line, is considering abortion.

THE KAISER COMES TO ORLANDO

You are having another one of your crazy nightmares and a big gaping mustachioed mouth is chasing you up seven post-Great-War decades of the Twentieth century. You're keeping ahead, but you come to a red light, and you have to stop because beyond is nothing, or heaven, or hell, so you mark time, waiting, and the gaping mouth is catching up to swallow you, you who have pledged allegiance to the Moose, and you collapse your dry knees like folding chairs, you break and bend them until you are under the kitchen table and, when you look up and out, you are back there again and they are charging at you across no-man's-land, spiked helmets and long thin bloodguttered bayonets, and in Orlando you go to the V.F.W. and live in a house where the sun burns back blindingly off the flung newspaper, its date a liar making you nearly a hundred, and you look up from your muddy trench, your long, bolt-action Springfield, its stock tangled under your trenchcoated arm, barrel aimed out toward them over sandbags, and with your free hand you pat your pet rat. Little black clouds form and vanish. You think they are like exploding eight balls. You hear *FIRE!* And your nerves jerk the trigger, while still petting the traitorous rat that scurries off. *OVER THE TOP!* You hear things crashing about you: the table, sugar bowl, coffee cups, a whole sideboard filled with dishes . . . And now a Great Power is holding you down and it is the cartoon face of the Hun, the fat rat-face and mustache of the Kaiser. He wants to eat you as he would a Belgian baby. Then you awake voiceless in England, a fire-breather, your elephant-nosed, goggle-eyed gas mask tangled, your sucking-for-breath, mustard-gassed lungs collapsed. Then you awaken in another hospital, in Orlando, Florida, seventy years later, and you are surrounded by strangers who say they are your family—they are strangers, of course, because you are still too young to marry, as Mother says you are, still too young for such responsibility, only a beardless boy from Hoboken in a slouch hat and brogans, an apprentice leatherworker commuting daily to Brooklyn, no scared-to-death doughboy in the Argonne and Belleau Wood, no Alzheimer's patient in a hospital bed in Orlando. And look, no jaywalker you! The light turns green for you to go!

THE THIN DISEASE

Nearly seven feet tall, a skeleton made of giant bird bones, a bird-cage rib-cage, his heart a little pulsing robin, Kwame from Ghana on the old Gold Coast was my best friend. Kwame had to reach down to tap me on my red head. "Dutch, we're going to cadge some drinks. You do the talking. Tell them I'm King Quazi of oilrich offshore Quaziland, and I can't speak English. Tell them my kingdom is ten miles long and a quarter mile wide, including beaches." Kwame had purple-grey skin and was so thin he looked like the shadow of a pole, but his head was large and noble, with cheekbones carved in slate, and royally crested with a pompadour befitting the son of a son of a king from the ancient West African Empire, though he was always churchmouse poor. We worked on the New York docks, offloading ships, on-loading trucks. He wasn't very strong. He drank a lot and bled from the rectum when he worked. They had to cut the grapes away. Like a daddy longlegs and a flat red beetle, we wobbled to a bar near St. Vincent's, a knot of stitches still in his new tight ass. He could ignore the pain for the booze. He put his arm over my shoulder. "Dutch, I'm going to die. I've got the thin disease. I'll never go back to Ghana." "Sure you will. You'll go back." There were good times yet. But he died. He died. He died. The white bed was empty but for a wave-crested, welted head, and limp hoses, some of which were black and leaked their fluids. Ghana was far away, a dream, but I was there, near, here, his friend, holding his hand, our funny different fingers entwined, though pulling apart.

THE WOULD-BE PIANIST

It always began with the would-be pianist coming into the room where the piano waited to be played and spinning the piano stool to a certain height, sitting down and lifting big hands above the keyboard; then a thinking pause, and down would come the hands that possessed passion but no skill and a terrible cacophony ensued, lasting about five minutes, at the end of which the hands turned into fists banging and banging in desperation, in frustration, in anger. "All you do is argue," cried the would-be pianist. "I never receive a kind note from you." The piano seemed to smile. It seemed that the piano tried to smile, but the smile, if achieved at all, appeared false, the smile of a piano that wants to please but is afraid. Bang came the fists, and now it seemed that the piano had more black keys than before but was trying harder than ever to smile. One leg had been kicked out from under it during an earlier session, but it stood firm now, propped by books on that weak leg. The would-be pianist knew of the weakness and kicked hard at the leg. Down went one end of the piano, with a rumble. "I'll teach you to mock me," cried the would-be pianist, opening the lid and slamming it shut. The piano uttered a sigh, like one who has given its last breath, given up the ghost, so to speak. This time the would-be pianist meant business. He called an antique store and told the dealer to come and get the devil of a piano, and good riddance. The would-be pianist was going to buy a brand new piano, one that could play, one that could respond to his dreams. The antique dealer fixed the piano's keys and repaired the leg so that it was stronger than ever. He sat down and played

Chopin's Fantaisie-Impromptu, finding, with some surprise, that the piano was in perfect tune. "How you survived such treatment," the antique dealer said, "is beyond me. You are a wonderful piano. A grand piano. I only wish I had known about you sooner—I'd have taken you away from that monster," and the piano, gleaming with polish, its keys shining and even, looked back at the antique dealer with true love and sang, bel canto, coloratura, like a diva.

"I HEAR YOU KNOCKING"

When all the matter of the universe finally finds a wall or floor or ceiling, the knocking will be enormous, and it will have to be heard, because, if there is a wall there is logically something on the other side of it, something that can hear it, wouldn't you say? I suppose you can't take this seriously, but it is in my peculiar chemistry to find it plausible. What could be on the other side of the wall? The dead? Well—the souls of the dead? It's hopeful. In such case, they would be sitting at God's feet and learning wisdom like a flock of hippies on a mountain learning from a guru. The wall would be dancing, of course, scientifically speaking, and the matter of the universe, made of mere ephemerons and faked to look like a facade, would not be half as solid as the wall of God's projective garden. Pascal would know how to penetrate it, though, thinking reed that he was, his thought would go through like wind-music; and that would be his great gambler's soul. *Oh, but God!* When all the matter of the universe finally finds a wall, the knocking will be truly mighty, like the beginning of B's Fifth!

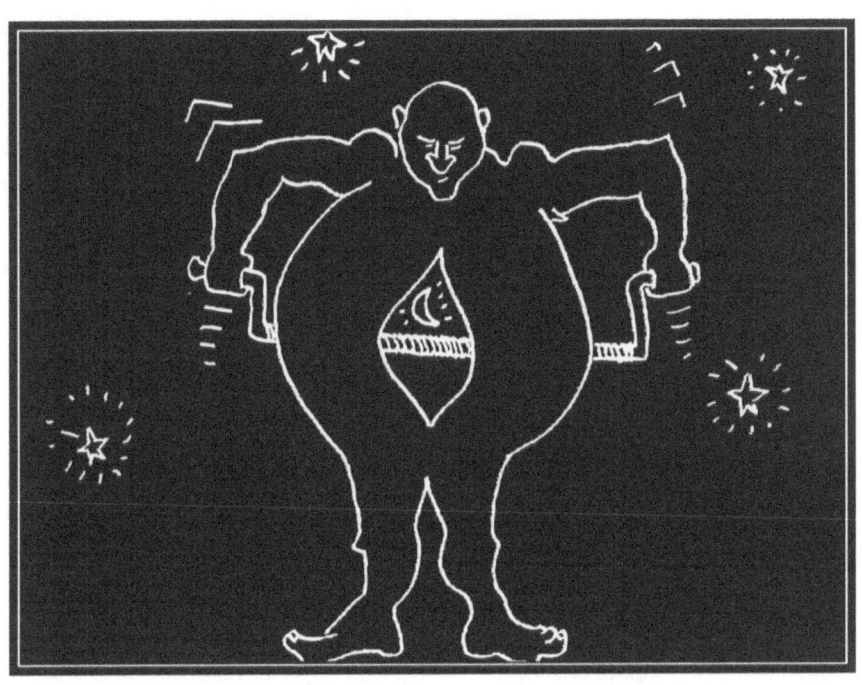

TWENTY-FIRST CENTURY MOLES

It was in the last century that moles came into their own. Of course it has always been true that they liked night life. But with the invention of the movie camera, moles began to listen to the music played with silent films. Of course they couldn't read the subtitles, but were able to pick up the dramatic impact of film from the vibes of the pounding piano. Nickelodeons were beyond them, but "The Great Train Robbery" got to them, and, for the first time in biological history, they strained to see. There are zoologists who insist that moles are still blind, but it is clear that the crowds at the Pantages and Grauman's Chinese are able to follow the floodlights to a nesting place in the dark; and, if able to follow the floodlights of the great openings and premiers of Hollywood, are certainly able to see the flickering lights on the screen. This is action-packed evolution. Now, any day or night of the week, you can see the public in multiplexes all over the world, munching five-dollar bags of popcorn and struggling to follow the plots of independent films. This I believe to be the final solution to the question of Intelligent Design and Darwinian theory. Dar wins!

WORLD'S STRONGEST MAN
CALLED UPON TO LIFT SLEEP

He was in the great tradition of Sandow, and so was intelligent as well as strong. He thought in terms of leverage and balance, not merely brute power. He would size things up, then think out a strategy for a lift. He resented being thought of as a mere freak of strength. He had studied engineering. This, he admitted, was to be his greatest challenge, and he thought for a long time before taking it on. The proposition posed many questions. Sleep has no handles. How do you get a grip on it? How do you train for such an event? Do you practice with naps, as you might with dumbbells for a barbell lift? And how many naps would be the equivalent of one sleep? Indeed, how long is a true sleep? And what of rem sleep? Do dreams and nightmares add to the weight? What does the average sleep weigh, and where can be found its specific gravity? He asked himself, "Are they asking me to lift the sleep of the world, or of just one person?" The rules must be made clear. His manager said not to worry, that lifting sleep sounded like a leadpipe cinch. "All you do is wake everyone up." But the world's strongest man replied that it would not be an easy task to wake everyone up at once, all over the world. It took more than sheer brute strength to be the world's strongest man; you had to have brains as well. You had to understand exactly what you were getting into. "You don't just lift things," he said. "But you have a point," he added, after a few minutes of thought. And he thought, Lifting sleep is the same as waking the sleepers. So I must find a way to wake everyone at once: and he decided to shake the Earth until everyone was awake. "That's my angle," he said. "I've got it." He had decided to push against the sky and run until he turned Earth's rotation backwards, causing such an uproar that everyone would wake up at once, thus lifting sleep the world over. He began pushing against the sky and running, digging his spikes into the soft earth, and lifting his knees like pistons. Then the world's strongest man's wife shook him and said, "Wake up, dear, you're having a nightmare." And he knew that he had lifted sleep from at least one person. Then the clock radio went on and he heard people talking, indicating that there were more from whom sleep had been lifted. "I think I've done it," he said, running about the house and pushing the sky in front of him. "We've overslept," said his wife. "You must hurry off to work." "Yes," he said, grabbing his briefcase, and he heeled out the front door—forgetting the car, which waited in the driveway, and down the block of suburban houses, and into the slow rise of the mountains, pushing the sky as he vanished into the distance.

PART IV

PUBLISHED BUT UNCOLLECTED

THIS MAN INSISTING UPON LIVING

How can I leave you with only one? If I give you nothing but that which I give what will protect you? Is this, do you think, only a rationalization, because I want to live? Is my heart as black as this typing ink? But I cannot leave you with only one! No, no, no! Nor can I leave you with only these, stamped and stamped, only these two: nor could I leave you with more if I had any more; no, not with three, if it were that three were here for me to leave, or even if I were lucky and had . . . but I cannot leave you with only two. Nor could I dream of leaving you with only these three. How would you survive; how could you ever get along? I must leave you with at least four. Do you think that four will be enough? No, I don't either; I'm sure you'll need more: five at the very least, yes, at least five. Oh, I am going to worry, worry so! I had better re-think this. Yes, I had better think more about this, for how could I live with myself if you didn't have enough to get by on? Yes, it had better be six, or seven, ten perhaps, and if I stay until tomorrow, I can, if I try, make it twenty or thirty, a thousand—yes! It must be a million: I must keep up my strength: perhaps I had better not go: I'm so busy.

THE THREATENING LETTER

The letter had an official look about it. I decided not to open it until I could sit down in the safety of my room, among familiar things, furnishings that offered confidence by their familiarity, advanced age and state of decay. I took it up to my room, gripped between thumb and forefinger and at left arm's length, as if I held the neck of a rattlesnake. People in the elevator watched as my hand shook and caused the envelope to rattle some mysterious and ominous document inside it. My aunt had served my unsuspecting uncle with divorce papers across the breakfast table one morning long ago. But I was already divorced, twice. My aunt had blamed my uncle for being unfaithful—and there was a question of money. I had never cheated on my wives, nor was money a problem. My crime had been my nervousness, which my wives asserted had caused them to become nervous wrecks themselves. And it was true that, as far as I knew, their nerves had been good until I married them, at which point they began to show signs of neurasthenia—impatience, tooth-grinding, insomnia, etc.—in point of fact the exact same conditions I have always suffered from. I dropped the letter on my cot and looked at it. It had landed address-down. I went to my closet and got out my vademecum, a slender walking stick of good birch with silver tip and handle, a device not only useful for aid in walking—I have a bad knee, acquired by banging it against another knee in the subway—but a handy tool of protection in case of an attempted mugging. Fortunately, I had never had to use it in the latter capacity. It was sheer luck that I hadn't been mugged by now, by which I mean by middle-age.

With the silver point of my walking stick I gingerly flipped the letter over, leaned the stick against the cot, and myself over to study the return address. My eyes were rheumy and I couldn't make out anything of the return address but some printing that suggested the blurred word *borough*, or *buro*, not clear at all. But, come to think of it, it suggested some dangerous department of government, did it not? I went to my desk, where I keep a pair of reading glasses and a magnifying glass, put the reading glasses on, being careful of my ears, and brought the magnifying glass back to the cot with me—but did I want to go on with this? Suppose it was a death notice, or suppose it was some official message involving an expense, a tax I had neglected to pay, or an assessment of some kind—what then? I stepped back from the cot and whacked the handle of my stick down upon the offending letter. It lay crinkled and bent in half, like a pale yellow claw gripping at the aggressive but escaped stick. Fear rose up through the floorboards, through the musty worn carpet, through the smooth soles of my patent leather shoes, and began to vibrate my legs, my torso, my whole body. My heart pounded until I could see it through my glistening shirt, heartshaped, leaving my chest, pounding more and more rapidly, thundering, now, in my ears. Fear had made it impossible to breathe. Something clanged in my head, a death knell, accompanied by the tintinnabulation of my mad fear. The roaring of my blood, the clanging in my head, the thundering of my room, made it impossible for me to think. I could only feel—hatred! Hatred for this pale claw that had intruded on my solitude, my small, ordered grace of life, and I beat at the letter, but it only bounced about on the cot as if jovial at the condition to which it had brought me. I remember nothing else, but I have been told that the landlord saw me from the door setting fire to the cover of the cot. I still don't know—was the letter from this institution?

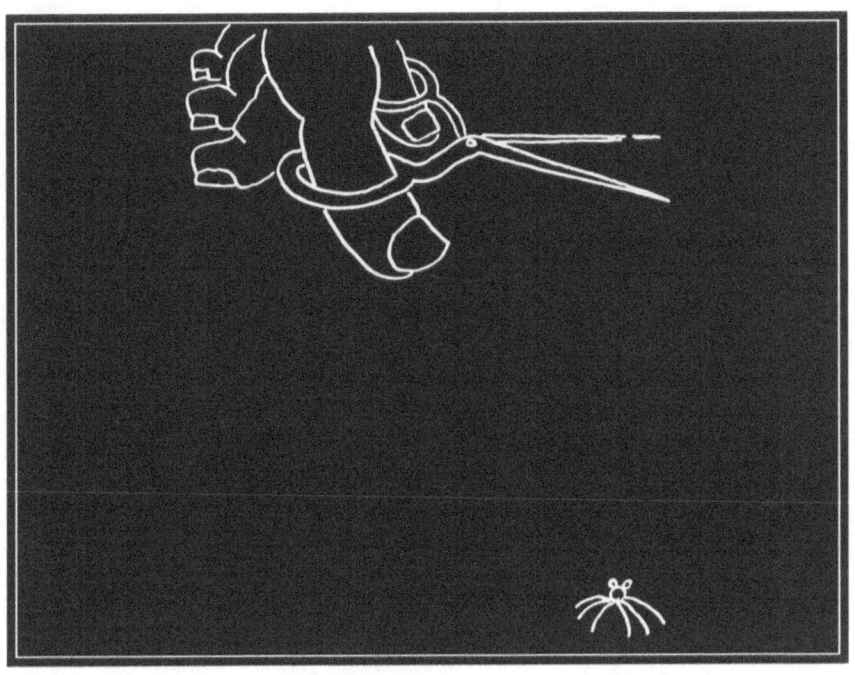

A MORBID ALBUM
from A Portable Chaos

> *So much of adolescence is an ill-defined dying,*
> *An intolerable waiting,*
> *A longing for another place and time,*
> *Another condition.*
> —Theodore Roethke

1. DENIAL

When you are about three feet tall, the gray streets of Philadelphia in winter are very long and tiring and slowly climb uphill toward a dark sky. His mother pulled him along. Where were they going? Had War Two begun yet? Their arms were empty. Not shopping? Was the Depression still on? Was there no money? Why were they walking, walking so far? He was beginning to get very cold. Then, on the empty street, a stranger appeared before them. He confronted them. His mother knew the man, yes, and they laughed together too high above him for him to have any idea what was funny, but something obviously was, or had been, for their laughter tinkled down upon him like sprightly snowflakes, like tinsel and sequins, a glittery sprinkling of fairy dust. He tried to get under it, between them, where it fell. His mother pulled him back and away, toward her own back. Then the man seized his mother in his arms and dipped her back toward where he waited and kissed her hard and long. It was wrong, wasn't it? Because this man was not his father. His father was up ahead somewhere, somewhere at the end of the long gray avenue, somewhere up several flights of stairs, in a small apartment that looked down on the avenue. It was wrong, wasn't it? Because his mother did not struggle to be free. Instead, she simply held him behind her, away from them. He could feel the strength of her grip. He thought he might cry, but wasn't sure if crying was the right thing to do. The man seemed to lift his mother off the pavement and to place her back on it, her high heels firm. She pulled him from behind her and around to her side. Her other hand held out to the man as he stepped back, back, and turned and went a little way, and stopped, and turned again, and waved, and blew her a kiss, and turned once again, and went on down the long slowly sinking avenue that his mother and he had just climbed. Who was that? he wanted to know. His mother pulled him forward up the hill. "Who was that?" he asked. His mother climbed on, pulling him along with one hand and wiping tears from her eyes with the other. "Mommy, who was that man?" His mother ignored him until he shouted his question at her. The question and its answer had become imperative, like the bearing down of traffic at the intersection. Finally his mother said, "What man?" He looked back and saw the receding figure of the man who had kissed his mother. He tugged his mother half around and pointed— "That man," he said. "I don't see any man," his mother said. "I haven't seen anyone since we began our walk, and neither have you." He looked back again, desperately, but the man was gone. "You see," said his mother. "There is no one on the street but us." She was lying, wasn't she, or could he not believe the evidence of his own eyes? From then on he struggled to keep his hand free of hers.

2. THE LETTER, 1942

His mother and father could not understand the extreme of his grief, for his father's other son was only half his brother, and had not existed in their lives but for letters and occasional photographs taken around the world where the war was, often next to his Wellington, or by a field tent, wearing his wings, a smiling twenty-year-old whom he, the child in a yard, thought must look the way he himself would look at twenty, and be a brave pilot and take up the war against Hitler and Tojo in his turn, not knowing that even wars do not last forever. How could the child be so devastated by the news, who barely knew of his half-brother's existence? How adults box things up the child could not know or believe. Hard rain. Rivers of rain, as when you look up through greenhouse glass on a rainy day, crossed his green eyes blotting out the blue dry sky overhead, and he told the rain of his grief and he told the blurred, ugly yard behind the city row house with its junked, warped furniture and strata of ripped linoleum, roses and geometry, and its wet, stalking cat along the old spiked wooden fence, run with rusted wire meant to throw yourself on, told the whole world, which was all the rain of tears out of his breathless, heaving chest, narrow as a chicken's, out of his pounding seven-year-old heart, and cowlicked hair, that was trapped by the four-sidedness of fence and could not fly with his grief as his brother the pilot had flown, whom he had never known. Let the child race pointlessly in circles, trapped in the square yard, and cry himself out. The letter was already over a year old and smeared with his father's few tears, sad horrible history, but must be set aside so that life could go on. "He'll get over it." "I never thought—" said his mother. "No, of course not," said his father. But the yard was sodden with the child's grief, whose head burned with hope against fact that a mistake had been made, that this fine brother was yet to come to him who had no one, whose loneliness could not be surmised by two wise parents, kept sane by callousing death and full of the hard world's rain.

3. A NICKEL IN THE SLOT

Late evening, once, on the crowded midway of a carnival, amidst it all, the gay calliope, the loud, scary, sucking sound of the polio fund-raising iron lung, the punctuating squeals of the other children with air, balloons, the pop, pop, pop of the rifles at the gallery, and the mad laughter of the funhouse, a seven-year-old came upon a fortune-telling machine, the illustrations of which showed the requirement of an Indian-head nickel in exchange for what children wish for most: Knowledge of the Future, which seems to give the feckless and the hapless power over it. He searched through his small change and found just such a nickel, plunged it in the slot of his future, and received in return a card the size of a standard business card with the following printed on it: *Act the Way you Want to Be and Soon You'll Be the Way you Act.* Little people take such advisements seriously, one might even say, with all their hearts; and so he tried to live that dream, and must assume that what he is, is what he desired to be, when he was an eager if short-sighted child.

4. SHINING

Like a spider on a thread, the eye dropped down on its optic nerve and drew up out of his range of vision. He was on his knees in a bar in Newark, shining shoes, maybe eight or nine years old. He sat between two men on stools whose heads were high above him. He was close to the level of the brass spittoon and the brass rail. They glittered with the reflection of the changing neon signs, but it was hard to see very well down there on the seat of the shoeshine box, hard to see anything but the whiteness of the eye, like an egg suspended on the cord that feeds the yoke. Some extraordinarily quick gesture of violence must have been employed. The shoes he was shining scrambled with the shoes he was about to shine. Crashing sounds, screaming, and he backed off to the wall behind him. A big scuffle of several men ensued. When he returned home late that night, his mother asked him if anything interesting had happened. "Have you ever seen an eye popped out?" he asked her, after stating his preference for the Campbell's Chicken Noodle soup over the Cream of Mushroom. He began counting his money, which he was saving for a bicycle, a Western Flyer. He was going to escape. He was going to become a Western Union boy.

5. IMPEDIMENTA

The rain flooded down the back steps and in under the old linoleum, floating it, with its sad faded roses, above the slab floor, an hallucination of a magic carpet, the backyard's muddy effluvium oozing into every corner and crevice and halfway down the hall to the bathroom, and making his mother cry for all her hard waxing work. His father, the superior drunk, had left them in this dump in Newark to go off selling his bullshit books in Buffalo, and to shack up with his beautiful vocabulary, quoth the raven, a bottle and a bimbo, and not to have to sit there with them, under the dripping pipes wrapped in soggy cardboard by the puke-green wall of bricks with a thousand holes in them for the bedbugs, roaches, and rumpled ringdings that came out at night and crawled all over them, biting, that swarmed like emigrating termites when the lights came on. The asbestos-insulated furnace belched, farted, and hummed outside their door, a jack-o'-lantern whose serrated teeth did not scare the rats, who warmed to him, in his furry gray suit that glowed in the dark, a giant rodent Golem. One could hear him breathing through the thin walls that divided the superintendent's apartment from the front basement, a pathed indoor junkyard. They had to wend their way out through that La Brea Tar Pit to get to the stairs that climbed and turned out to the street, where they would peep up to see if anybody out there would notice where they were coming from, which was out from among the dented old metal cans full of raw garbage, and what peculiar species of spelunker they were—what Untouchables were surreptitiously seeking light and air. He lied about his age and became a Western Union boy, having shoeshined his way to the top, saved his money and bought a bicycle, a Western Flyer, O Icarus! He found his mother a pretty little apartment high over a pizza joint, and they moved up into the air and the smell of baking dough. His timid mother was shocked at such derring-do, daring to fly so high, so near to the sun; and, for a while, they were happy. But his father came home and said, "This place is too expensive." We must get another sump-pump dump to superintend. "Another nice basement that drips piss?" The boy asked, and added, "No, I can afford to pay this rent, as I have been doing for some time now. Now stick with me on this one, Mom." *But we better do what your father thinks best*, she whispered; and he said to himself—"That's it, never again," as he helped to carry their embarrassing paltry possessions—"Impedimenta" his father called them—through the streets. His father led the way like a brass hat, soused and self-important, his mother followed him into nothing but worse, with a "Wither-thou-goest" and a last wistful look up over the pizza parlor at their window of opportunity, a dutiful wife of the Fifties, and he planned his escape.

MOONTIME

The Greeks measured Earth by its shadow on the moon. Thoreau said, Time is a stream I go fishing in. Ford said, History is the bunk. Sumerian writing, done on clay tablets, shows about 2000 pictographic signs. The moon is a bad woman because she is very romantic. We all know the trouble romance can get you in. I am romantic tonight, amorous with the moon. O how many leaves lay scattered? I guess thousands, and I have a study that agrees with me. When you pay for a study, you get what you want. Therefore, all studies are romantic and have a dark side like the moon. Theodora, the Byzantine empress, died in 548, one of a kind. Her death was a big relief to some of her subjects. Five years later disastrous earthquakes shook the entire world. The house I live in was built much later. I leave the actual count to you. The first water-driven mechanical clock was constructed in Peking in 1090, the wrist watch around the turn of the Twentieth century. I've got a digital that I can read in the dark. I can also read the chained and sailing moon from here. Its glyphs of pox say the odds are against us.

ARGONAUTS
from A Portable Chaos

>*for Edmund Bosch*

>*Verde que te quiero verde.*
>*Verde viento. Verdes ramas.*
>   —Lorca

We stripped down to whatever we intended to wear as swimming togs and sat down on the hot stone to enjoy some cold beer from sweating cans before taking the first plunge. There was a small concrete bridge down below the deeper pool and a pickup truck whizzed by over it, otherwise no sound but water and talk and laughter, shrill cries from the kids. Below the bridge the water dropped in a steep fall and then, after a rushing meander, into the lake. The lake was very large and dark and it was claimed that Good Peter, a phantom Oneida chief, beat an ominous tattoo upon a tom-tom out there at night. He lamented—*The voice of the white birds from every quarter cried out, You have lost your country! You have lost your country!* His whole tribe had been wiped out by the white man and he was out for justice (scientists said the night rumblings were made by natural gas, a less impressive explanation). After the beer we took a plunge in the water and then Ed had an idea. He had heard that somewhere upstream was a great waterfall, one that fell for perhaps a hundred feet—not a Niagara, but a fair cataract and it was supposedly located in a canyon of considerable beauty—and would I like to hike up the stream with him to find it. I said I would and we started off together up the shallows. Ed had been roughing it in a woodland way now for several years and moved along at a good pace over the slippery rocks, sometimes through the water, sometimes along the bank, but more often through the water, because the bank was quite steep most of the way and often it was non-existent, only a sheer wall of rock in its place. He looked a mythological figure of a man, tall and broad and beefy of shoulder, red and bushily bearded, sharp-eyed, visored cap pulled low for the slanting sun: he moved sure-footed as a goat—or not quite that, for he did slip occasionally, but even a mountain goat might have slipped on these watery stones. I kept apace about twenty yards behind and it took my whole attention focused upon where I was next to step to keep me from dropping farther behind. I was about thirty-five, Ed nearly forty, so we were no longer boys and this delicate goat-walking on watery stone was an effort, of the body but then more of the will. Where were we going? Where? And why? Why make the effort? Back at the lower pools near the bridge there was rest on the hot stone with beer, kept cold by the cold purling water and the shade of the rock over it; so why this little odyssey, this minor quest? Why be Argonauts? When I looked up Ed had disappeared ahead of me and I saw a long gently rising glassy piece of water, reflecting mountains, bushes, trees and below the crazily slanting mountains, bushes and trees, all the little gems half buried in a slippery silt, as if the flow of the water had discovered a sunken treasure, brightly colored arrowheads, axes, peacepipe fixtures, as yet all un-manufactured—the raw material of a stone culture, the proud stuff of the phantom drummer of the lake and casting over it all, over the reflected, layered escarpments, over the faint tiny rock flowers, little bits of bright blue, scarlet, and gold, fool's gold, the reflected sky and the mysterious shadows of unseen birds, wind-caught leaves, swaying lazy branches and I wondered where was Ed: had I fallen so far behind in this amazing world, was all this sudden glare and shadow too much to be accepted, was I no longer any part of it, that could flow with it all at will, or without will, without the consultation with will, as I imagined the red shadows who were men and women that had flashed here once had been able to do? But then I saw Ed, as I came wading kneedeep in water around the long bend and he was standing on a rock his arms akimbo and breathing hard; I could see his back heave; he turned to me and motioned and pointed up through the trees and I followed his gaze and saw deeply hidden a small cabin grayed by weather. Ed grinned and pointed. "A poet!" he called and turned to his task of getting from one rock to another, the mountain goat. Again we came upon a small waterfall with a sharp declivity and we had to work our way around it up the steep embankment of black mud and moss. Our feet and fingers ripped and upheaved the fine smooth moss as we scurried, a bit fearful of taking a long uncontrollable slide backwards and on to the jutting rocks and then we were able to drop down again into the cool water at the top of the fall and the mud was washed from our feet and I dipped my hands in the water and rinsed the mud from my knees. The water here was only about four inches deep but stepping into it I was alarmed by its pressure and for an instant thought it might overtopple me and send me headlong down the fall to crumple my poor head on the rocks below, but I was learning already that to deal with nature one must relax: it is the only "safe" way. I had already learned not to fight the stone under my bruised feet but to put down a foot with all its muscles loose and to let it find its shape on the earth: otherwise it will not be accepted and rejection is the danger. Had I begun sliding down the muddy bank I should have forced myself to relax, to go limp and to accept my fate and I was already winning a faith that helped me believe that I should have merely slid over those jutty rocks like a piece of mossy mud and gone on sliding down and down and down the great fall under the bridge and meandered, making with my body some mystic hieroglyphs in the water, until I fell gently into the lake without hurt. I might have passed my wife and children and called to them to wait. I might have been ushered into that dark frothy water by low drums at twilight. Would life be so bad? But now we came upon an exceedingly long and narrow place which, except for the fact that it was all moss and stone and gurgling, rushing water and the fact that it was so terribly deep a trench in the high mountains, reminded me of one of those canals that city workmen dig in which to lay pipe for sewers and I felt like a workman on break now as Ed and I sat, panting, and smoked a cigarette and looked up the long alley at the fall there, perhaps a hundred yards ahead and Ed said "What do you think? Should we keep on going?" I don't know what it was that made me sense the larger fall beyond the smaller, perhaps it was some accurate unconscious reading of the lay of the land, or something vibratory in the rocks, but it seemed something else which I am forced to say was a kind of indescribable sensation: I sensed a great booming mystery that was also a sort of magical silence beyond and I said yes, let's go on. This was a treacherous place, for the water was deep and rushing with great, foaming force down its narrow confines and there was just moss-slippery rock edging steeply up into the thickest bramble and tangle of green life I could remember having seen: but somehow we found our way onto a wide open flat place and the water was gentle again, almost still but for a slight observable upper purling, a rippling and it was all open here, wide and open again and I felt as if I had been in a tunnel and now I was out again in the open. But there was still a sense of being low and it must have been due to the sense of height ahead, because we were already quite high up: we had come nearly two miles steadily upward and that was from a high place itself. Yes, the feeling of being low must have been because of the great height I sensed ahead. Or because of the mountains rising all around me: or because the azure and pink-streaked sky still seemed to be so high above. I had an image of men casting for trout with long, flexible poles, men with wading boots and colorful flies pinned all over their hats: pipes in their mouths. And when I looked up Ed was gone—gone again! And for all I had learned my feet were badly bruised, cut even and I would have been limping had I been walking on soft grass, so I had to take these ridiculous delicate little steps, like a baby's steps and I'd probably be left so far behind I'd be ashamed to be such a tenderfoot. And I wondered, with my Zen Master, what were the punishments of them that serve the Evil One, of those who cannot make their living except through violence to Being. And I saw Ed, ahead, standing in the center of a great open place and the water up to his ankles and he pointed up, crying over the natural sounds "Look! Look!" And I took one last look at my poor wretched feet to see that they were well placed on the slippery-as-ice rocks and looked up to where he pointed and saw an over-awing escarpment circling round us in deep beautiful folds of rock and placed us in a kind of canyon. And my feet slipped and up they went most idiotically into the air and down I went plunging and thrashing and laughing like a fool, but I kept my plaid slouch hat that Ed had given me above the water and a bit of my forehead and I came up making an absurd joke of how the beauty of the place had knocked me over and Ed at first afraid I had hurt myself began to laugh and I looked in my hat and best of all my smokes were still dry, and so I scampered on in the sun drying off and caught up with Ed and right around a bend in this enormous place—there was the waterfall. We pulled ourselves up on some rocks and Ed lit a joint and passed it to me. We looked around and I thought I must never let the details of this quest blur in memory. I must get right back to Ed's ramshackle old farmhouse and scribe the magic of it all. Oh—The waterfall came down for fifty feet or more, then hit an odd rock and fell out like an opening fan across itself; so it was like two falls, one down, one crossing that, like translucent lovers entwined and undulating and above them, below a deep blue twilit heaven, a great cliff hung, weighted with trees. I knew a mystic place when I saw one; a tabernacle. So did Ed. And an Oneida Chief stood on the cliff in full regalia. He was smiling.

AN ANTIQUARY OF THE FUTURE

We have nothing like it, dating, I should say, from the mid-Twenty-first Century. Look at those hairdos. The clothes. They just don't make them like that anymore. Here, shake it. It won't break. It can't go away anymore. It is all told. But you see, they still have a touch of the old moonglow? And look at those sunbelt tans. Notice that when you shake it, no snow drifts, only it glows with a kind of sunlight and there are white puffs of cloud in that light blue background. Clearly, it was a beautiful day. But it rained later, see, and the sky turned dark blue, and then nearly black, so that you can hardly see the lovers, and, when it lightens again, time after time, they are different, older and sadder, but kinder. Then shake it again, and there they are again, full of young lust, full of hormones and mean selfhood of the worst sort. It's sad. Dates back to the ancients, the primitives. What's it worth? You can't put a price on a dream like this. It's a classic.

ABOUT THE AUTHOR

E.M. Schorb is a prize-winning poet, novelist, and short story writer. His *Murderer's Day* was awarded the Verna Emery Poetry Prize and published by Purdue University Press; his collection, *Time and Fevers*, was the recipient of the Writer's Digest International Self-Published Award for Poetry and also an Eric Hoffer Award. Most recently, *Words in Passing,* was published by The New Formalist Press. Other works include *50 Poems,* Hill House New York, *Reflections in a Doubtful I,* White Violet Press, *The Journey and Related Poems,* Aldrich Press, *The Ideologues and Other Retrospective Poems,* Aldrich Press, and *The Poor Boy,* Dragon's Teeth Press, Living Poets Series. The title poem, "The Poor Boy," was awarded the International Keats Poetry Prize by London Literary Editions, Ltd., judged by Howard Sergeant. Schorb's novel, *Paradise Square,* received the Grand Prize for Fiction from the International eBook Award Foundation at the Frankfurt Book Fair. *A Portable Chaos* was the First Prize Winner of the Eric Hoffer Award for Fiction. His most recent novel, *Resurgius: A Sixties Sex Comedy,* about which X.J. Kennedy has written: "Resurgius, unique though it is, strikes me as belonging to the very league as the comic gems of Evelyn Waugh and Nathaniel West," was published by Rainy Day Reads Publishing. But Schorb maintains that he is first and foremost a poet, and his poetry has appeared in numerous publications, here and abroad.

www.ingramcontent.com/pod-product-compliance
Lightning Source LLC
Chambersburg PA
CBHW031413290426
44110CB00011B/367